£0.50   £1.25

D0727128

ROBERT HENRYSON

To
JAMES PARKER OAKDEN
in gratitude

ROBERT HENRYSON

SELECTED POEMS

---

edited with an introduction by
W. R. J. Barron

FYFIELD BOOKS
Carcanet   Manchester

First Published in 1981 by
Carcanet New Press Limited
330 Corn Exchange Buildings
Manchester M4 3BG

Printed in Great Britain by Billings, Guildford

CONTENTS

INTRODUCTION

APRIL in the north can be a cruel month:

> . . . in middis of the Lent,
> Shouris of haill can fra the north discend,
> That scantly fra the cauld I miht defend.
>
> I mend the fire and beikit me about,
> Than tuik ane drink my spreitis to comfort,
> And armit me weill fra the cauld thairout.

It might be Burns, or Fergusson, or MacDiarmid rather than Henryson; they shared a climate and an idiom which set them apart from their fellow-poets to the south. Perhaps, also, the distinct perspective which led Henryson to choose spring, the season which provided setting, atmosphere, and basic metaphor for so many medieval poems of idealised love, as the starting point for his own treatment of the destructive effects of a deceptive love in *The Testament of Cresseid*. For his adoption of such conventions, amongst other reasons, he has been labelled a 'Scottish Chaucerian'; his distinctive use of them may ultimately suggest that the former adjective must dominate the latter.

Of Henryson the man very little is certainly known, despite his fame in his own time. Dunbar includes him in his *Lament* on the ravages of death amongst the *makaris* of his generation:

> In Dunfermelyne he hes done roune
> With Maister Robert Henrisoun.

Since he was most probably already dead when the poem was written, *c*. 1505, and died, according to less reliable evidence, 'very old', he may well have been born quite early in the second quarter of the previous century (see Wood, xi-xiii). The title 'Maister' suggests that he was an M.A., possibly of a continental university, since there is no record of his graduation at St Andrews or Glasgow and Anglo-Scottish relations in the fifteenth century probably debarred him from Oxford and Cambridge. The title pages of two early printed editions of poems by Henryson style him 'Schoolmaster of Dunfermline', and the other scanty records persistently associate him with the town where there was a grammar school connected with the ancient Benedictine abbey (see S.T.S., I, xxiii-xxv). The abbey, founded *c*. 1074 by St Margaret, wife of Malcolm Canmore, its guest-house now converted into a royal palace, had become an important centre of political, religious and educational administration, and its grammar school was amongst the oldest and most important in Scotland (see MacQueen, 16-17). Dunfermline was no rural backwater and Henryson, on the evidence of his poems alone, no half-educated village dominie.

The Scotland of his maturity was a troubled country under a weak king, James III (1460-88); in his old age, under James IV (1488-1513), a more orderly and prosperous place. The growing prosperity showed itself in the comfort of the towns and the wealth of their burgesses; the richness of the new-built castles, churches and abbeys; the three universities founded within the century and the many flourishing grammar schools dating, in some instances, from the eleventh century. Scottish schools and universities shared the same common medieval curriculum in which the basic subjects, grammar, rhetoric and logic, were taught through the medium of the Latin classics and contemporary commentaries upon them. But in a century in which many Scottish teachers had attended continental universities, when trade and diplomacy carried Scots to the markets of the Low Countries and the papal Curia at Rome, something of the new Christian humanism had perhaps already reached their remote country (see MacQueen, 1-15).

Since the transition from Middle Ages to Renaissance was a process of fusion and mutation, the literary effects of the new cultural influence were not immediately apparent. The Scots poetry of the fifteenth and early sixteenth century was still medieval, particularly in its aptitude for story-telling and its acceptance of an ordered universe, divinely created and controlled, which gave perspective and meaning to all experience, human or animal, comic or tragic (see Muir, 10-11). It was also predominantly 'Chaucerian' in that it still found validity in the poetic forms, the rhetorical usages, the common European themes which Chaucer's genius had given universal currency in the English language. But it was a European tradition in which Chaucer inspired Henryson and his younger contemporaries, William Dunbar and Gavin Douglas, to work; and one to which the Auld Alliance with France against the power of England had given the Scottish *makars* direct access ever since the end of the thirteenth century (see Wittig, 62-3). That Scotland's continental outlook exposed them equally readily to the influence of the Renaissance is apparent in the aureate diction, learned and Latinate, of all three, in Douglas's epic *Eneados*, and in the subjects and sources of Henryson's three major poems (see Fox [1970], 170-1). If it is less obvious in his treatment of them that is, perhaps, because he was not a court poet.

Orpheus and Erudices

We know nothing of his patrons—if, indeed, he had any—nor of the order in which he wrote the poems, but on the evidence of poetic maturity *Orpheus and Erudices* may well have been an early work. The story it tells of Orpheus' descent into the underworld to rescue his wife Eurydice by charming the powers of hell with his music, and how he lost her again by breaking the condition that he should not look at her until they had reached the upper world, was familiar in various medieval versions of the classical original. Henryson could therefore take the narrative very much for granted, using it as little more than a thread on which to string various poetic show-pieces: on the names and functions of the muses; the lament of Orpheus for his lost love; his journey through the heavenly spheres in search of her and what he learnt there of the art of music; the topography of hell and the torments of its inhabitants, mythical, historical, and contemporary. The resultant mixture has puzzled modern critics who judge the erratic structure, rapid narrative interrupted by apparently irrelevant excursus, as evidence of lack of poetic purpose and the basic cause of the poem's failure.

But it is misleading to judge a medieval poem in terms of modern expectations. At one level at least Henryson's poetic purpose is manifest. In his immediate source, Boethius' *Consolation of Philosophy*, the story is used to resolve the paradoxical dilemma into which Boethius has been led by reasoning that 'happiness is the highest good, to be equated with God, and that as God is omnipotent, and yet cannot do evil, evil does not exist' (MacQueen, 29). The co-existence of good and evil is illustrated by his teacher, Philosophy, whose interpretation of the myth gives to Eurydice a dual role: as the thought which, like man in his ideal function seeking the highest

11

good through reason, Orpheus sought to lead to the light above; and also as the desire which caused him, like fallible man subject to illusion and appetite, to turn back towards the dark. 'As one who desired the highest good, Orpheus rescued Eurydice; as one subject to illusion, he made the mistake by which he lost her again' (MacQueen, 30). Henryson clearly accepted this allegorical interpretation of the myth, following in his *moralitas* the standard commentary of Nicholas Trevet. In keeping with contemporary theology, dominated by the ideas of Thomas Aquinas, Trevet interpreted Orpheus as the intellectual power of the soul, Eurydice as its sensual appetite which, fleeing from Virtue (the shepherd Aristaeus), is stung by the serpent Sensuality and falls into the dominion of hell, from which the intellectual power is capable of rescuing her.

Though Henryson's *moralitas* does its patient duty by Trevet's allegorical interpretation, there is a paucity of invention in its application to the narrative, a lack of zest in the plodding couplets which make it difficult to accept as the poet's primary interest in *Orpheus and Erudices*. It is equally unconvincing to see the narrative as no more than a vehicle for a display of classical knowledge, a catalogue of the wonders of hell and the heavens, as 'popular' entertainments without organic function in the poem (see Speirs, 30-33). They can be given organic function by a thorough-going allegorical interpretation (see MacQueen, 31-44); but in some cases only by unjustified assumptions on their derivation from allegorical contexts, or by extrapolation from the *moralitas*. 'Two inferences are possible: either Henryson has wavered uneasily between an allegorical and a non-allegorical method, or . . . he intended the *moralitas* to provide an optional and added level of meaning, not the obligatory key to the entire poem' (Wright, 46-7).

There was, in effect, another Orpheus tradition in the Middle Ages, oral rather than literary, popular rather than learned, which associated him with David, the magical musician who played in the wilderness, and with Christ the Good Shepherd who prophesied that the lion should lie down with the lamb. The thirteenth century *Sir Orfeo* shows him as a wise king, a divinely-inspired musician who conquers the ruler of the otherworld, but also as a loving, suffering human being. The influence of this romance tradition upon Henryson is evident in his tracing of the hero's lineage to establish him as a worthy leader of men, elaborating the refinement of his musical skill amongst the spheres in preparation for his triumph in charming the spirits of hell, stressing his human reaction to the sufferings of the souls in torment, and substituting forgetfulness in a moment of joy for carnal passion as the cause of the backward glance by which he lost Eurydice (see Louis, 646-53). It was Orpheus' ability to suffer as a man and his power to express his feelings as a poet which most attracted Henryson to the myth, to judge from the quality of his own verse in the hero's lament for his lost love (134-181), in the barren Scottish landscape of his journey through hell (261-316), and in the final comment on the bitter-sweet nature of human love which provides the real *moralitas* of the poem:

> 'What art thou, luf, how sall I the diffine?
> Bitter and sweit, cruell and merciable,
> Plesand to sum, till uthir plaint and pine,
> Till sum constant, till uther variable.
> Hard is thy law, thy bandis unbrekable;
> Wha serviss the, thoht he be never so trewe,
> Perchance sumtime he sall have caus to rew.'   (401-7)

The Morall Fabillis

The moral intention of Henryson's longest work, proclaimed in its title, was inherent in the tradition of the fable which, from Aesop onwards, used the lives of beasts and birds as a pattern of human life reduced to an easily comprehensible scale and set against an unquestioned Christian morality (see Muir, 14). Man's shortcomings are spelt out in the *moralitas*, to which the narrative forms an illustrative *exemplum*, with an explicitness which the modern mind finds dull and obvious, redeemed only by its manifest sincerity. The tales are accepted, without reservation, for their narrative skill, the concrete, realistic, sharply visualised world in which they are set, the humour of their cleverly contrived situations, the couthy wit of their dialogue. But truth to life can never be the sole criterion of any literary form in which animals act and speak as men, and the medieval reader would instinctively assume a symbolic intention: 'the final value, in each fable, is not the mortal world but some absolute, whether perfect justice, divine wisdom, or eternal life' (Fox, 356).

That Henryson saw his literary function as a dual one, and a figurative technique as the means of achieving both aims, is made clear in the opening stanza of the *Fables*:

> Thoht feinyeit fabils of ald poetre
> Be not al grunded upon truth, yit than
> Thair polite termes of sweit rhetore
> Riht plesand ar unto the eir of man;
> And als the caus that thay first began
> Wes to repreif the haill misleving
> Of man be figure of ane uther thing. (1-7)

His aim is to provide pleasure and through it moral correction; his means are all the arts of poetry, from the figural technique which presents animals like men as a reminder that, though divinely endowed with greater potential, men are often no better than animals, to the figures of speech which are most potent when most pleasing. The means may be merely fictive (*feinyeit fabils*), but the end is truth. Medieval rhetoric taught the art of variation and elaboration, and the remainder of the Prologue is a complex, highly organised, yet apparently casual expansion of this initial statement, expressing the relationship of fable and moral in changing metaphors of earth and corn, nutshell and kernel, which suggest the natural universe we are about to enter. On a wider scale, the thirteen fables which follow fulfil the same rhetorical principle, constantly varying that relationship, and elaborating the fictional element with differing degrees of realism and emotional conviction (see Toliver,302-3). In each case Henryson's use of his source material has been highly selective: always expanding, but concentrating in different cases upon sharpening the narrative focus, increasing verisimilitude, or heightening humour (see Macdonald, 101).

The opening 'Taill of the Cok and the Jasp' is deceptively simple. The *moralitas* interprets the cock who neglected the jewel scratched up in the dirt because it was not edible as the stubborn fool who, blinded by appetite, rejects wisdom. Yet the simplistic moral is undercut by the solidity with which the world of the barnyard is established by the elaborate rhetoric—ludicrous in a bird, yet persuasive—in which the cock justifies his attitude, and by his association with humanity in the persons of those housemaids by whose negligence such a jewel may be swept away and lost. In the words of the cock we hear both the special pleading of fallible mankind engaged in self-justification and a sympathetic statement of natural, rational, material values (see Fox, 341-8). If our response is ambivalent, the rigidity of the *moralitas* challenges our response to absolute values in the face of our common humanity as we recognised it in the cock.

The 'Taill of the Uponlandis Mous and the Burges Mous' seems to lose sight of moral perspective in the detailed realism of its mimic world of mice. But by endowing his mice with all the petty vices, the greed and snobbery, the timidity and pretension of the shabby-genteel, Henryson repeatedly evokes their human counterparts (see Tillotson, 1-2). At the same time, by contrasts of scale which constantly remind us of their petty size and by showing them subject to poverty and prosperity, in security and adversity, he reminds us of the fickleness of fortune and the malign forces before which man without God must crouch in fear. When, therefore, the *moralitas* recommends the simple life because *the cat cummis,* there is an ironic undertone to its heroic rhetoric which mocks the pettiness of human desires.

The 'Taill of Shir Chantecleir and the Foxe' inevitably challenges comparison with Chaucer's *Nun's Priest's Tale*, but where Chaucer leaves the reader to seek the moral fruit amongst a great deal of entertaining but seemingly irrelevant chaff, Henryson's spare and rapid narration illustrates the theme of the fable, the danger of that self-deluding vanity which lays one open to flattery, to which the fox proves just as susceptible as his victim the cock. Even in what seems incidental, elements of barnyard realism or comic relief, the moral theme is being richly harmonised. The fox's affection for the cock's late father and his tender care of him on his deathbed has an ominous irony in view of his well-known appetite for barnyard fowl; and the sincerity of the hens' elaborate lament for their lost mate is undermined by their complaints of his sexual incapacity and their lust to replace him with a more potent paramour (see Fox [1970], 173-6). The tone ranges widely, from the impressively rhetorical to the comically colloquial, but throughout death provides a foil to hypocrisy and self-importance.

Expert narration, comic invention and embarrassingly exact parody of human speech and manner again dominate in 'The Tod's Confessioun'. But the very features which attract our sympathy for the fox—his man-to-man urbanity, the blatancy of his observance of the forms while flouting the spirit of Penance, the wit of his superficial self-deception—and persuade us to take his 'tragedy' seriously, are just those which bring the disaster upon him. His shameless tempting of fate, as he suns his well-filled belly, brings the arrow of retribution from the bow of the goatherd whose stolen kid he had re-baptised as *Shir Salmond*, and he dies unhallowed through his own neglect of the sacraments. Humanly, one regrets a good joke gone sour; 'but if someone is always spoiling a joke, the total allegory and the *moralitas* show the reason to be that one cannot play with the fire of his mortal condition without getting burned' (Toliver, 303).

The moral core of the fable tradition is only seriously neglected in 'The Parliament of Beistis' with its conscious imitation of the debate in Chaucer's *Parlement of Foules*. It allows Henryson to display his rhetorical ability in the formalities of legal pageantry and his technical skill in the alliterative catalogue of beasts. But the trial and summary execution of the fox provide too abrupt a descent to the traditional parody of human folly after a long proem which seemed to promise a serious allegory of human justice. Possibly in an age when the making and execution of law were more intimately connected, and evidence of royal justice in operation at the humblest levels was socially reassuring, the plot would appear more unified and the *moralitas* less contrived.

By contrast, 'The Preiching of the Swallow' is the most organic as well as the most original of all Henryson's fables. A simple narrative of carefree birds who ignore the swallow's repeated warnings of the danger in a field of flax while it grows, ripens, is harvested and woven into the nets in which they are snared and killed. And an obvious *moralitas* showing how the Devil traps and kills the souls of men enmeshed in the sins which spring from wicked thoughts he sows in their minds, while they ignore the warning voice of the preacher. But this is only the most explicit level of the wider theme of prudence, announced in the opening lines and richly harmonised

16

in every element of the poem. In the pre-narrative proem, one third of the whole, an apparently rambling discourse on the perfect prudence of God to whom all time, past, present and future, is eternally present, and on his control of the universe, perfectly ordered in space and time for the benefit of all his creatures, rebukes the folly of man, subject to time and fortune yet arrogantly confident in the ability of natural reason to cope with changes he cannot foresee (see Burrow,30-5). Tracing the seasons from summer to spring in a cycle of hope, the proem leads us from abstract philosophy to concrete instance in the fable of the birds, whose natural, instinctive, but purblind, enjoyment of the moment through spring and summer, rebutting the passionate rhetoric of the swallow's warnings with the pat truisms of proverbial wisdom, makes inevitable their death in winter; a tragi-comedy of blind folly in a benign universe. In turning away from the higher good of God's design in self-willed indulgence, the birds exemplify the fundamental theme of Henryson's *Fables*: 'the conflict between man's carnal and spiritual sides, . . . between the natural and the supernatural worlds, between the actual and the ideal' (Fox, 356).

The Testament of Cresseid

Henryson's greatest poem has perhaps been too little studied in relation to his other work, too much in relation to Chaucer's *Troilus and Criseyde*. He clearly expected his audience to know Chaucer's masterpiece and plays upon that knowledge, often ironically, in his own. He takes up the narrative where Chaucer left it and deals exclusively with the punishment of Cresseid for her desertion of Troilus; but this need not imply that where Chaucer used their history to examine human love in relation to the *caritas* which binds his creation to a loving creator, Henryson, as a narrow-minded Scottish puritan, saw that relationship only in terms of divine retribution upon a traitor to love. The balance of morality and humanity in his other poems may rather suggest that here too Henryson is attempting to bring out the fundamental meaning of a pre-existing narrative and make his own assessment of the values traditionally associated with it (see Fox [1968], 21-2).

Certainly his poem could not contrast more strongly with Chaucer's in scale, in structure and in poetic method. With extreme narrative economy it concentrates on the crises in the action, crucial moments of realisation and recognition: Cresseid's fatal outburst against the gods (116-40), her departure to the lazar-house on being stricken with leprosy (344-406), and her last meeting with Troilus when neither recognises the other (484-539). As with the few stanzas of linking narration elsewhere, the crises are outlined with a starkness and emotional restraint which works upon the feelings by its very understatement:

> When Diomed had all his appetite,
> And mair, fulfillit of this fair lady,   (71-2)

'The two words "and mair" suggest a terrible weight of satiety and humiliation' (Cruttwell, 186). All the more potent, in such a context, are the occasional moments of emphatic assertion, leaving no circumstance to the imagination, as when Cresseid, rejected by Diomed:

> Riht prively, but fellowship, on fute,
> Disagysit, passit far out of the town   (94-5)

Such narrative compression is not only possible but fitting because the essential action of Cresseid's tragedy is over before Henryson takes up the story. Only the final downturn of Fortune's wheel remains and its relentless movement through betrayal, prostitution, disease, bitter self-knowledge and death is less significant in itself than in its ironic relationship to the fortunate past (see Spearing, 183-4).

That relationship is evoked by the passages of lyrical elaboration, rhetorical amplification amongst narrative compression, which accompany each of the crises of action. Cresseid's *Complaint* (407-69), marked by its distinctive stanza, is at the heart of the poem, expressing her bitterness and regret at the loss of her beauty and the ease and honour which it had commanded. At its close comes her outburst of self-accusation (540-74) with its lyrical refrain:

> O fals Cresseid and trew kniht Troilus!

Between them lies the true development of the poem; an interior development in Cresseid's acceptance of her fate and understanding of its cause, for which the narrative proper provides only the circumstantial context.

The function of the other lyric interlude, Cresseid's vision of the deities associated with the seven planets (141-343), has puzzled critics. Beneath the magnificence with which they are described there are repeated hints of their malign and destructive power, providing an external explanation for the vengeful punishment which her outburst against Venus and Cupid brings upon her (see Spearing, 172-80). But what is the source of their power? Are they irrational forces operating upon the lives of men by blind fortune, or instruments of God's will? If the former, Cresseid has offended against a purely secular code of love and is punished by the pagan deities who govern it, with the thematic implication that lovers should beware the inherent fickleness of women and women the fickleness of fortune (see Noll, 23-5). If the latter, then Cresseid's blasphemy is a sin against God, her leprosy the retribution of a strict providence untempered by mercy, and the theme an unresolved conflict between respect for divine judgement and sympathy for human suffering (see Duncan, 131-5). Recent criticism, however, sees the moral issue as subservient to the theme of human suffering in which the gods personify the impersonal planetary influences which bring misfortune upon mankind, including the misfortune of his own folly: 'Gods who are powerful and cruel are set against human beings who are impotent, foolish and wicked, but who demand our emotional involvement, our compassion, because they are capable of suffering and the gods are not' (Spearing, 190).

In this interpretation the focus of the poem is not upon Cresseid as a sinner brought to repentance and regeneration, but as one who, in her *Complaint*, sees herself as the helpless plaything of forces of anarchy and mutability, yet comes, in the end, to accept her bitter lot and acknowledge her own responsibility for it; 'she discovers that salvation lies in regarding her history as that of a free, if culpable, individual, whilst despair lies in viewing it as the unhappy chronicle of a passive, if inoffensive, victim' (Tristram, 149). In presenting Cresseid's tragedy as an extreme example of a cruel, if deserved, fate, Henryson was dealing in a particular case with issues of transience and mutability which preoccupied the later Middle Ages. Much of this generalisation of the particular is implied by the proem (1-42) which presents the poem as the work of an elderly man whom time has turned away from love to a book by the fire, himself an image of the operation of mutability upon the human passions. The frost in

April which drives him from contemplation of Venus rising in the evening sky to the reading of literature, the record of human experience, is a chill reminder of the cycles of nature and the cycle of the Christian year bringing the lenten season of repentance and the spiritual rebirth of Easter. If the showers of hail, the coming of night with Venus dominant in a frosty sky, the purifying blast of the northern wind imply a harsh view of the fragment of human experience which is to follow, it is perhaps inspired less by moral condemnation than by that realistic clarity of vision by which men come to a knowledge of things in their own natures (see Tristram, 147-8).

The Cresseid who, in ignorance of her own nature, raged against the transience of beauty and the mutability of fortune is brought to recognise, in the reiterated *ubi sunt* of her *Complaint*, the common lot of mortal man. Her recognition tacitly rejects Fortune as man's master; but she is still not reconciled to the natural order. Reconciliation comes through suffering and through love. The love of Troilus, expressed in an act of compassion inspired by the shadow of a loved face in a hideously deformed leper, brings bitter recognition of her own falsity and acceptance of man's responsibility for his own destiny:

> 'Nane but myself as now I will accuse.'   (574)

According to a seventeenth century authority, as Henryson lay dying he was told by an old woman, the local witch, that if he would walk three times round a rowan tree in his garden repeating 'Whikey tree, whikey tree, take away this flux from me' it would cure the dysentery from which he suffered. The old man, objecting that there was snow on the ground, pointed to an oak table in his room and said: "Gude dame, I pray ye tell me if it would not do as well if I repeated thrice theis words: 'Oken burd, oken burd, garre me shit a hard turd'" (See S.T.S., I, ciii). The story may be apocryphal, but it fits well the image of Henryson which his poetry projects: a realist who viewed the doctrines and values of his age with detachment but without cynicism, and expressed his view of them with gentle wit, touched with irony, in an idiom rooted in colloquial speech.

Despite its native idiom his poetry does not treat any specifically Scottish subject; yet in each of his major poems the landscape and climate of Scotland impinge, colouring romance and pastoral with shades of northern gray, hardening moral judgements with a touch of frost. There is nothing of the literary rebel or the cultural back-woodsman in Henryson's choice of story-matter, literary format, or rhetorical convention, but each is handled with an individuality which sets it apart from the commonplaces of the age. All his major subjects were inherited—a fact which would have recommended him to medieval readers; his originality showed itself not in radical re-interpretation, but in a profound sense of situation and a sharp eye for detail.

As his age required, he was a moralist and a teacher, but he did not use his art primarily to preach a conventional morality. By exploiting the poetic potential of his material he gave it a validity in its own right which reinforced its didactic function. The moral force of his work is not in the formal intellectual summary of the *moralitas* but in the truth to experience which the writing conveys. The fact that the smug satisfaction of a fox crammed with forbidden delicacies, the panic of birds caught in the fowler's net, the self-disgust of a famous beauty stricken with leprosy can still speak to the human condition today suggests that Henryson worked not through moral argument but through emotional conviction, independent of the literary conventions of a particular age.

The poetic idiom which is the medium of that conviction has too often been praised for one feature only, the humorous effects created by colloquial Scots in a formal context. It is perhaps the last feature which would have struck his northern contemporaries familiar with Scots as a literary language based on the speech of ordinary men, but enriched with the aureate vocabulary which it inherited with the rhetorical conventions and intellectual concepts of Western Europe. They would rather have noticed that he had a fondness for Chaucer's rhyme royal and have admired the skill and variety with which he handled it, evolving an expanded and enriched stanza form of his own for the formal laments of Orpheus and Cresseid—and parodying his own invention in the lamentation of the bereaved hens in the 'Taill of Shir Chantecleir'! But they would also have noticed and admired his command of the alliterative medium, which Scottish poets inherited from their neighbours to the south and west and they in turn from their Anglo-Saxon ancestors, and his use of it for stately formality as well as comic over-emphasis.

It is this ability to command a variety of voices, traditional and personal, which allows him to write with such economy; no major poem of the Middle Ages is so compact as the *Testament of Cresseid*. It is not merely that he can compress so much action into a single stanza, but that by concentrating in each upon an instant of time, sharply visualised, he reveals the narrative in vivid flashes which endure in the mind during the static interludes when he works upon our emotions by a very different, highly coherent, lyrical diction. The juxtaposing of contrasting styles he may have learnt from Chaucer, but the flashes of action coupled with emotional indirection are reminiscent of the ballads. His virtuosity is always subservient to his poetic purpose; even the occasional pieces, with their complex internal rhyming and insistent alliteration, never lose sight of their serious themes of pestilence, old age and death.

Though he wears his learning lightly—except when ostentation is part of his poetic purpose—Henryson was clearly no village ballad-monger. His vocabulary is rich and his use of it discreet and funct-ional. Like Chaucer, he can exploit the complexity of meaning in a word: *pain*, used for the penalty inflicted on Cresseid by the gods, is reiterated in its modern sense to express her suffering. Like him, he can marshal aureate terms impressively:

> O Prince preclair, this cair cotidiane,
> We the exhort, distort it in exile!

He can catch a visual image in a vivid phrase:

> The harrowis hoppand in the saweris trace;

and sketch character in a line of dialogue:

> The lark, lauhand, the swallow thus couth scorne,
> And said sho fishit lang before the net;
> 'The barne is eith to busk that is unborne;'

But he is perhaps most himself when he reworks a convention in his native idiom:

> Sine cummis ver, when winter is away,
> The secretar of somer with his sell,
> When columby up-keikis throu the clay,
> Whilk fleit wes befoir with froistes fell.

22

The mavis and the merle beginnis to mell;
The lark on loft, with uther birdis haill,
Than drawis furth fra derne over down and daill.
The rhetoric is European, but the voice is Scots.

TEXTUAL NOTE

Of the works generally attributed to Henryson, both his major poems, just under half of his collection of fables, and four of the thirteen minor pieces are included here. His works survive in a number of manuscripts and early prints listed and described in S.T.S., I, pp. xlv-lxxxii; II, pp. vii-xviii; in Wood, pp. xix-xxx and, more briefly, in Elliott, pp. xix-xxi. The source of each text is indicated in the Notes; minor textual emendations have been made without comment. Since the intention has been to make Henryson's work available to the general reader with an interest in early poetry, the texts are presented as far as possible in conformity with modern usage in matters of punctuation, capitalisation and word-division. The following typographical and spelling modifications have been made: þ appears as *th*, ʒ as *y*, and *z* (for scribal ʒ) also as *y*; the use of *i/y, i/j, u/v/w* and *ie/y* is generally adapted to modern conventions; *quh* has been simplified to *wh*, *sch* to *ch*, *ch* to *h* and final *ff* to *f*. It is hoped that with these modifications the text will be more readily comprehensible, while retaining something of the distinctive character of Henryson's Middle Scots.

GLOSSES

The glossing of unfamilar words and obscure forms has been restricted to the minimum consistent with reasonably rapid and easy reading of the text. Inevitably it will seem excessive to some readers, insufficient to others. The latter may find that their difficulties spring less from Henryson's vocabulary than his poetic exploitation of it, which, it has been assumed, they would wish to appreciate for themselves. Glossed terms repeated in the immediate context are not re-glossed. The frequently-used words listed below are not normally glossed in context:

als: also, as so
ane: a, one
aneub: enough
anis: once, ones (pl.)
attour: about, above, over
auld: old
bide: dwell, tarry
bidand: awaiting
but: without
can (couth, culd, etc.): does, did , etc., as an auxiliary with other verbs
cauld: cold, coldness
deir: dearly, precious

do (dois, doit, dude, etc.): as an auxiliary with other verbs
forwhy: because, since
gar: cause, make
hait: hot
man, mon(e): must
noht, nouht: not, nothing
or: ere, before
sall: shall
sely: poor, foolish
sho: she
sic: such
sicker: sure, safe, good

sine: then, again
suld, sould: ought, should
sumdeill: somewhat
tent: care, heed
thir: these
wait: know, watch
wedder: weather
whair: where(by), with which
whais: whose
whilk: who, which
whill: until
wox: grow, became

SELECT BIBLIOGRAPHY

Abbreviations used in the Introduction and Notes are indicated in the margin.

EDITIONS

S.T.S. / *The Poems of Robert Henryson*, ed. G. Gregory Smith, Scottish Text Society, I 55, 58, 64, Edinburgh, 1906-14.

WOOD / *The Poems and Fables of Robert Henryson*, ed. H. Harvey Wood, Edinburgh, 1933. (Rev. ed., 1958)

ELLIOTT / *Robert Henryson: Poems*, ed. Charles Elliott (Clarendon Medieval and Tudor Series), Oxford, 1963.

FOX (1968). / *Testament of Cresseid*, ed. Denton Fox (Nelson's Medieval and Renaissance Library), London, 1968.

STUDIES

Bennett, J.A.W., 'Henryson's *Testament*: a flawed masterpiece', *Scottish Literary Journal*, I (1974), 5-16.

Burrow, J.A., 'Henryson: *The Preaching of the Swallow*', *Essays in Criticism*, XXV (1975), 25-37.

Cruttwell, P., 'Two Scots Poets: Dunbar and Henryson' in *The Age of Chaucer*, ed. B. Ford (*The Pelican Guide to English Literature*, I), Penguin Books, 1961, 175-87.

Duncan, D., 'Henryson's *Testament of Cresseid*', *Essays in Criticism*, XI (1961), 128-35.

Fox, D., 'Henryson's *Fables*', *ELH*, XXIX (1962), 337-56.

Fox, D. (1970), 'The Scottish Chaucerians' in *Chaucer and Chaucerians*, ed. D.S. Brewer (Nelson's University Paperbacks), London, 1970, 164-200.

Grierson, H.J.C., 'Robert Henryson', *Aberdeen University Review*, XXI (1933-4), 203-12.

Harth, S., 'Henryson Reinterpreted', *Essays in Criticism*, XI (1961), 471-80.

Kinghorn, A.M., 'The Minor Poems of Henryson', *Studies in Scottish Literature*, III (1965-6), 30-40.

Louis, K.R.G., 'Robert Henryson's *Orpheus and Eurydice* and the Orpheus Traditions of the Middle Ages', *Speculum*, XLI (1966), 643-55.

Macdonald, D., 'Narrative Art in Henryson's *Fables*', *Studies in Scottish Literature*, III (1965-6), 101-13.

MacQueen, J., *Robert Henryson: A study of the Major Narrative Poems*, Oxford, 1967.

Muir, E., 'Robert Henryson' in *Essays on Literature and Society*, revised edition, London, 1965, 10-21.

Noll, D.L., '*The Testament of Cresseid*: Are Christian Interpretations Valid?' *Studies in Scottish Literature*, IX (1971-2), 16-25.

Spearing, A.C., 'Conciseness and *The Testament of Cresseid*' in *Criticism and Medieval Poetry*, second edition, London (1972), 157-92.

Speirs, J., 'Robert Henryson' in *The Scots Literary Tradition*, London, 1940, 11-34.

Stearns, M.Y., *Robert Henryson*, New York, 1949.

Tillotson, G., 'The 'Fables' of Robert Henryson' in *Essays in Criticism and Research*, Cambridge, 1942, 1-4.

Tillyard, E.M.W., 'Henryson: *The Testament of Cresseid*' in *Five Poems: 1470-1870*, London, 1948, 5-29.

Toliver, H.E., 'Robert Henryson: From *Moralitas* to Irony' *English Studies*, XLVI (1965), 300-9.

Tristram, P., *Figures of Life and Death in Medieval English Literature*, London, 1976.

Wittig, K., *The Scottish Tradition in Literature*, Edinburgh, 1958.

Wright, D.A., 'Henryson's *Orpheus and Eurydice* and the Tradition of the Muses', *Medium Aevum*, XL (1971), 41-7.

THE TESTAMENT OF CRESSEID

Ane dooly sessoun to ane cairfull dite	dreary, poem
Suld correspond, and be equivalent.	
Riht sa it wes when I began to write	
This tragedy; the wedder riht fervent,	severe
When Aries, in middis of the Lent,	
Shouris of haill can fra the north discend,	
That scantly fra the cauld I miht defend.	(7)

Yit nevertheles within mine oratur	oratory
I stude, when Titan had his bemis briht	
Withdrawin doun and sylit under cure;	hidden, cover
And fair Venus, the beuty of the niht,	
Uprais, and set unto the west full riht	
Hir golden face, in oppositioun	
Of God Phebus, direct discending doun.	(14)

Throuout the glas hir bemis brast sa fair	
That I miht se on every side me by;	
The northin wind had purifyit the air,	
And shed the misty cloudis fra the sky;	swept
The froist freisit, the blastis bitterly	
Fra Pole Artick come whisling loud and shill,	shrilly
And causit me remufe aganis my will.	(21)

For I traistit that Venus, luifis quene,	
To whome sumtime I heht obedience,	vowed
My faidit hart of lufe sho wald mak grene,	
And therupon, with humbill reverence;	
I thoht to pray hir hie magnificence;	
Bot for greit cald as than I lattit was,	prevented
And in my chalmer to the fire can pas.	chamber

Thoht lufe be hait, yit in ane man of age	(29)
It kendillis noht sa sone as in youtheid,	
Of whome the blude is flowing in ane rage;	

And in the auld the curage doif and deid,   *desire, quenched*
Of whilk the fire outward is best remeid:
To help be phisike whair that nature faillit,
I am expert, for baith I have assailit.   *tried*

I mend the fire and beikit me about,   (36)
Than tuik ane drink my spreitis to comfort,
And armit me weill fra the cauld thairout.
To cut the winter niht and mak it short,
I tuik ane quair—and left all uther sport—   *book*
Written be worthy Chaucer glorious,
Of fair Creisseid and lusty Troilus.   (42)

And thair I fand, efter that Diomeid
Ressavit had that lady briht of hew,
How Troilus neir out of wit abraid   *went*
And weipit soir, with visage paill of hew;
For whilk wanhope his teiris can renew,   *despair*
Whill Esperus rejoisit him agane: *Evening Star(=hope)*
Thus while in joy he levit, while in pane.   (49)

Of hir behest he had greit comforting,   *promise*
Traisting to Troy that sho suld mak retour,
Whilk he desirit maist of eirdly thing,
Forwhy sho was his only paramour.
Bot when he saw passit baith day and hour
Of hir ganecome, than sorrow can oppres   *return*
His wofull hart in cair and hevines.   (56)

Of his distres me neidis noht reheirs,
For worthy Chauceir, in the samin buik,
In gudely termis and in joly veirs,
Compilit hes his cairis, wha will luik.
To brek my sleip ane uther quair I tuik,
In whilk I fand the fatall desteny
Of fair Cresseid, that endit wretchitly.   (63)

Wha wait gif all that Chauceir wrait was trew?   knows
Nor I wait noht gif this narratioun
Be authoreist, or fenyeit of the new   authentic
Be sum poeit, throu his inventioun
Maid to report the lamentatioun
And wofull end of this lusty Creisseid.
And what distres sho thoillit, and what deid.   suffered, death

When Diomed had all his appetite,   (71)
And mair, fulfillit of this fair lady,
Upon ane uther he set his haill delite,
And send to hir ane libell of repudy,   writ of divorce
And hir excludit fra his company.
Than desolait sho walkit up and down,
And, sum men, sayis, into the court, commoun.   promiscuous

O fair Creisseid, the flour and *A per se*   paragon
Of Troy and Grece, how was thou fortunait   predestined
To change in filth all thy feminity,   (80)
And be with fleschely lust sa maculait,   defiled
And go amang the Grekis air and lait,
So giglotlike, takand thy foull plesance!   like a strumpet
I have piety thou suld fall sic mischance!   (84)

Yit nevertheles, whatever men deme or say
In scornefull langage of thy brukkilnes,   frailty
I sall excuse, als far furth as I may,
Thy womanheid, thy wisdome and fairnes,
The whilk Fortoun hes put to sic distres
As hir pleisit, and nathing throu the gilt
Of the—throu wickit langage to be spilt!   (91)

This fair lady, in this wise destitute
Of all comfort and consolatioun,
Riht prively, but fellowship, on fute,   without
Disagysit, passit far out of the town
Ane mile or twa, unto ane mansioun

29

Beildit full gay, whair hir father Calchas
Whilk than amang the Greikis dwelland was. (98)

When he hir saw, the caus he can inquire
Of hir cumming; sho said, sihing full soir,
'Fra Diomeid had gottin his desire
He wox wery and wald of me no moir.'
Quod Calchas, 'Douhter, weip thou not thairfoir;
Peraventure all cummis for the best.
Welcum to me; thou art full deir ane gest!' (105)

This auld Calchas, efter the law was tho,
Wes keiper of the tempill, as ane preist,
In whilk Venus and his sone Cupido
War honourit, and his chalmer was thame neist;   *adjacent to*
To whilk Cresseid, with baill aneuh in breist,   *sorrow*
Usit to pas, hir prayeris for to say;
Whill at the last, upon ane solempne day, (112)

As custome was, the pepill far and neir,
Befoir the none, unto the tempill went
With sacrifice, devoit in thair maneir;
Bot still Cresseid, hevy in hir intent,   *sad*
Into the kirk wald not hirself present,
For giving of the pepill ony deming   *suspicion*
Of hir expuls fra Diomeid the king; (119)

Bot past into ane secreit orature,
Whair sho miht weip hir wofull desteny.
Behind hir bak sho cloisit fast the dure,
And on hir kneis bair fell down in hy;
Upon Venus and Cupide angerly
Sho cryit out, and said on this same wise:
'Allace that ever I maid you sacrifice! (126)

'Ye gave me anis ane devine responsaill
That I suld be the flour of luif in Troy;

Now am I maid ane unworthy outwaill,   *cast-off*
And all in cair translatit is my joy.
Wha sall me gyde? Wha sall me now convoy,
Sen I fra Diomeid and nobill Troilus,   (132)
Am clene excludit, as abject odious?   *outcast*

'O fals Cupide, is nane to wyte bot thou,   *blame*
And thy mother, of lufe the blind Goddes!
Ye causit me alwayis understand and trow
The seid of lufe was sawin in my face,   *sown*
And ay grew grene throu your supply and grace.
Bot now, allace, that seid with froist is slane,
And I fra luiferis left, and all forlane.'   *abandoned*

When this was said, doun in ane extasy,   (141)
Ravischit in spreit, intill ane dreame sho fell,
And be apperance hard, whair sho did lie,
Cupide the king ringand ane silver bell,
Whilk men miht heir fra hevin unto hell;
At whais sound befoir Cupide appeiris
The sevin planetis, discending fra thair spheiris,   (147)

Whilk hes power of all thing generabill   *created*
To reull and steir be their greit influence,
Wedder and wind, and coursis variabill.
And first of all, Saturne gave his sentence,
Whilk gave to Cupide litill reverence,
Bot as ane busteous churle on his maneir,   (153)
Come crabitly, with auster luik and cheir.   *stern*

His face fronsit, his lire was like the leid,   *wrinkled, hue*
His teith chatterit and cheverit with the chin,
His ene droupit, how sonkin in his heaid;   *downcast*
Out of his nois the meldrop fast can rin,
With lippis bla, and cheikis leine and thin;
The ice-shoklis that fra his hair down hang   *icicles*
Was wonder greit, and as ane speir als lang.   (161)

Atouir his belt his liart lokkis lay   over, grizzled
Felterit unfair, ovirfret with froistis hoir;   matted
His garmound and his gyis full gay of gray;   attire
His widderit weid fra him the wind out woir;   blew
Ane busteous bow within his hand he boir;
Under his girdill ane flashe of felloun flanis,   sheaf of deadly
Fedderit with ice and heidit with hailstanis.   [arrows

Than Juppiter, riht fair and amiabill,   (169)
God of the starnis in the firmament,
And nureis to all thing generabill;   fosterer
Fra his father Saturne far different,
With burely face and browis briht and brent,   lofty
Upon his heid ane garland wonder gay,
Of flouris fair, as it had bene in May.   (175)

His voice was cleir, as cristall wer his ene,
As goldin wire sa glitterand was his hair;
His garmound and his gyis full gay of grene,
With golden listis gilt on every gair;   hems, seam
Ane burely brand about his middill bair;
In his riht hand he had ane groundin speir,
Of his father the wraith fra us to weir.   .   ward off

Nixt efter him came Mars the God of ire,   (183)
Of strife, debait, and all dissensioun,
To chide and feht, als feirs as ony fire;
In hard harnes, hewmound, and habirgeoun,   helmet, mail-coat
And on his hanche ane rousty fell fachioun,   cruel scimitar
And in his hand he had ane rousty sword;
Writhing his face with mony angry word.   (189)

Shaikand his sword, befoir Cupide he come,
With reid visage and grisly glowrand ene;
And at his mouth ane bullar stude of fome,   bubble
Like to ane bair whetting his tuskis kene;   boar
Riht tuilyeour-like, but temperance in tene,   quarrelsomely, anger

32

Ane horne he blew with mony bosteous brag,
Whilk all this warld with weir hes maid to wag.   (196)

Than fair Phebus, lanterne and lamp of liht
Of man and beist, baith frute and flourishing,
Tender nureis, and banisher of niht;
And of the warld causing, be his moving
And influence, life in all eirdly thing,
Without comfort of whome, of force to noht
Must all ga die that in this warld is wroht.   (203)

As king royall he raid upon his chair,   chariot
The whilk Phaeton gydit sum time unriht;
The brihtnes of his face, when it was bair,
Nane miht behald for peirsing of his siht;
This goldin cart with firy bemis briht
Four yokkit steidis, full different of hew,
But bait or tiring throu the spheiris drew.   (210)

The first was soir, with mane als reid as rois,   sorrel
Callit Eoye into the orient;
The secund steid to name heht Ethios,
Whitly and paill, and sumdeill ascendent;
The third Peros, riht hait and riht fervent;
The feird was blak, callit Philology,
Whilk rollis Phebus down into the sey.   (217)

Venus was thair present, that Goddes gay,
Hir sonnis querrel for to defend, and mak   cause
Hir awin complaint, cled in ane nice array,   odd
The ane half grene, the uther half sabill black;
White hair as gold, kemmit and shed abak;
Bot in hir face semit greit variance,
Whiles perfite treuth and whiles inconstance.   (224)

Under smiling sho was dissimulait,
Provocative with blenkis amorous,   glances

33

And suddanely changit and alterait,
Angry as ony serpent vennemous,
Riht pungitive with wordis odious;   *stinging*
Thus variant sho was, wha list tak keip,   *note*
With ane eye lauh, and with the uther weip.   (231)

In taikning that all fleshely paramour,
Whilk Venus hes in reull and governance,
Is sumtime sweit, sumtime bitter and sour,
Riht unstabill and full of variance,
Mingit with cairfull joy and fals plesance,
Now hait, now cauld, now blyith, now full of wo,
Now grene as leif, now widderit and ago.   (238)

With buik in hand than come Mercurius,
Riht eloquent and full of rethory,
With polite termis and delicious,
With pen and ink to report all reddy,
Setting sangis and singand merily;
His hude was reid, heklit atour his crown,   *fringed*
Like to ane poeit of the auld fassoun.   (245)

Boxis he bair with fine electuairis,   *medicinal syrups*
And sugerit syropis for digestioun,
Spicis belangand to the pothecairis,
With mony hailsum sweit confectioun;
Doctour in phisick, cled in ane skarlot gown,
And furrit weill, as sic ane auht to be;
Honest and gude, and not ane word culd lie.   (252)

Nixt efter him come Lady Cynthia,
The last of all, and swiftest in hir spheir;
Of colour blak, buskit with hornis twa,
And in the niht sho listis best appeir;
Haw as the leid, of colour nathing cleir,   *livid*
For all hir liht sho borrowis at hir brother
Titan, for of hirself sho hes nane uther.   (259)

Hir gise was gray and full of spottis blak,
And on hir breist ane churle paintit full evin,
Beirand ane bunche of thornis on his bak,
Whilk for his thift miht clim na nar the hevin.
Thus when thay gadderit war, thir Goddes sevin,
Mercurius thay cheisit with ane assent
To be foirspeikar in the parliament.   (266)

Wha had bene thair and liken for to heir
His facound toung and termis exquisite,   eloquent
Of rhetorick the prettick he miht leir,   practice, learn
In breif sermone ane pregnant sentence write.
Befoir Cupide veiling his cap a lite,
Speiris the caus of that vocatioun,
And he anone shew his intentioun.   (273)

'Lo', quod Cupide, 'wha will blaspheme the name
Of his awin god, outher in word or deid,
To all goddis he dois baith lak and shame,   disrespect
And suld have bitter panis to his meid.   reward
I say this by yone wretchit Cresseid,
The whilk throu me was sumtime flour of lufe,
Me and my mother starkly can reprufe,   (280)

'Saying of hir greit infelicity
I was the caus, and my mother Venus,
Ane blind goddes hir cald, that miht not se,
With slander and defame injurious.
Thus hir leving unclene and lecherous
Sho wald returne on me and my mother,   blame
To whome I shew my grace abone all uther.   (287)

'And sen ye ar all sevin deificait,   deified
Participant of devine sapience,
This greit injure done to our hie estait
Me think with pane we suld mak recompence;
Was never to goddes done sic violence.

35

As weill for you, as for myself I say;
Thairfoir ga help to revenge, I you pray!'   (294)

Mercurius to Cupide gave answeir
And said,'Shir King, my counsall is that ye
Refer you to the hiest planeit heir,
And tak to him the lawest of degre,
The pane of Cresseid for to modify: assess
As God Saturne, with him tak Cynthia.'
'I am content,' quod he, 'to tak thay twa.'   (301)

Than thus proceidit Saturne and the Mone,
When thay the mater ripely had degest: considered
For the dispite to Cupide sho had done,
And to Venus, oppin and manifest,
In all hir life with pane to be opprest,
And torment sair with seiknes incurabill,
And to all lovers be abhominabill.   (308)

This duleful sentence Saturne tuik on hand,
And passit down whair cairfull Cresseid lay,
And on hir heid he laid ane frosty wand;
Than lawfully on this wise can he say:
'Thy greit fairnes, and all thy beuty gay,
Thy wantoun blude, and eik thy goldin hair,
Heir I exclude fra the for evermair.   (315)

'I change thy mirth into melancholy,
Whilk is the mother of all pensiveness;
Thy moisture and thy heit in cald and dry;
Thine insolence, thy play and wantones
To greit diseis; thy pomp and thy riches   distress
In mortall neid; and greit penurity
Thou suffer sall, and as ane beggar die.'   (322)

O cruell Saturne, fraward and angry,   ill-humoured
Hard is thy dome and to malitious!

36

On fair Cresseid why hes thou na mercy,
Whilk was sa sweit, gentill and amorous?
Withdraw thy sentence, and be gracious—
As thou was never; so shawis thou thy deid,
Ane wraikfull sentence gevin on fair Crisseid.   vengeful

Than Cynthia, when Saturne past away,   (330)
Out of hir sait discendit down belive,   quickly
And red ane bill on Cresseid whair sho lay,
Contening this sentence diffinitive:
'Fra heit of body I the now deprive,
And to thy seiknes sall be na recure,   cure
Bot in dolour thy dayis to indure.   (336)

'Thy cristall ene minglit with blude I mak;
Thy voice sa cleir, unplesand, hoir and hace;   rough, hoarse
Thy lusty lire ovirspred with spottis blak,   complexion
And lumpis haw appeirand in thy face;
Whair thou cummis, ilk man sall fle the place.
This sall thou go begging fra hous to hous,   thus
With cop and clapper like ane lazarous.'   (343)

This dooly dreame, this ugly visioun
Broht to ane end, Cresseid fra it awoik,
And all that court and convocatioun
Vanischit away; than rais sho up and tuik
Ane poleist glas, and hir shaddow culd luik;
And when sho saw hir face sa deformait,
Gif sho in hart was wa aneuh, God wait!   (350)

Weiping full sair, 'Lo, what it is', quod she,
'With fraward langage for to mufe and steir   provoke
Our craibit goddis; and sa is sene on me!
My blaspheming now have I boht full deir;
All eirdly joy and mirth I set areir.
Allace, this day! allace, this wofull tide
When I began with my goddis for to chide!'   (357)

37

Be this was said, ane child come fra the hall
To warne Cresseid the supper was reddy;
First knokkit at the dure, and sine culd call,
'Madame, your father biddis you cum in hy:
He hes mervell sa lang on grouf ye lie,   prostrate
And sayis, your prayers bene to lang sumdeill;
The goddis wait all your intent full weill.'   know

Quod sho, 'Fair childe, ga to my father deir   (365)
And pray him cum to speik with me anone.'
And sa he did, and said, 'Douhter, what cheir?'
'Allace!' quod sho, 'Father, my mirth is gone!'
'How sa?' quod he; and sho can all expone,
As I haue tauld, the vengeance and the wraik
For hir trepas Cupide on hir culd tak.   (371)

He luikit on hir ugly lipper face,
The whilk befor was white as lilly flour;
Wringand his handis, oftimes he said, allace
That he had levit to se that wofull hour!
For he knew weill that thair was na succour
To hir seiknes, and that doublit his pane;
Thus was thair cair aneuh betwix thame twane.   (378)

When thay togidder murnit had full lang,
Quod Cresseid: 'Father, I wald not be kend;
Thairfoir in secreit wise ye let me gang
Unto yone hospitall at the townis end;
And thidder sum meit for cherity me send
To leif upon; for all mirth in this eird
Is fra me gane—sic is my wickit weird!'   cruel lot

Than in ane mantill and ane baver hat,   beaver-fur
With cop and clapper, wonder prively,   (387)
He opnit ane secreit yet and out thairat   door
Convoyit hir, that na man suld espy,
Unto ane village half ane mile thairby;

Deliverit hir in at the spittaill hous,
And dayly sent hir part of his almous.   (392)

Sum knew hir weill, and sum had na knawledge
Of hir, becaus sho was sa deformait
With bylis blak ovirspred in hir visage,
And hir fair colour faidit and alterait.
Yit thay presumit, for hir hie regrait   distress
And still murning, sho was of nobill kin;
With better will thairfoir they tuik hir in.   (397)

The day passit and Phebus went to rest
The cloudis blak ovirwhelmit all the sky.
God wait gif Cresseid was ane sorrowfull gest,
Seing that uncouth fair and harbery.   lodging
But meit or drink sho dressit hir to lie
In ane dark corner of the hous allone;
And on this wise, weiping, sho maid her mone: (406)

The Complaint of Cresseid

'O sop of sorrow, sonkin into cair!   (one) soaked in
O cative Creisseid! For now and evermair   wretched
Gane is thy joy and all thy mirth in eird;
Of all blyithnes now art thou blaiknit bair;   made destitute
Thair is na salve may saif the of thy sair!   heal
Fell is thy fortoun, wickit is thy weird;
Thy blis is baneist, and thy baill on breird!   misery is growing
Under the eirth, God gif I gravin wer,   grant, buried
Whair nane of Grece nor yit of Troy miht heird!   hear it

'Whair is thy chalmer wantounly besene,   adorned
With burely bed and bankouris brouderit bene;   splendid
Spicis and wine to thy collatioun,   [coverlets
The coupis all of cold and silver shene,   (419)
The sweitmeitis, servit in plaittis clene,

39

With saipheron sals of ane gud sessoun;   sauce
Thy gay garmentis with mony gudely gown,
Thy plesand lawn pinnit with goldin prene?
All is areir, thy greit royall renown!   gone

'Whair is thy garding with thir greissis gay,   plants
And freshe flowris, whilk the quene Floray   (426)
Had paintit plesandly in every pane,   plot
Whair thou was wont full merily in May
To walk and tak the dew be it was day,   as soon as
And heir the merle and mavis mony ane,
With ladyis fair in carrolling to gane
And se the royall rinkis in their array,   folk
In garmentis gay garnischit on every grane? smallest part

'Thy greit triumphand fame and hie honour,   (434)
Whair thou was callit of eirdly wihtis flour,   mortals
All is decayit, thy weird is welterit so;   reversed
Thy hie estait is turnit in darknes dour.
This lipper ludge tak for thy burely bour,
And for thy bed tak now ane bunche of stro;
For waillit wine and meitis thou had tho   choice
Tak moulit breid, peirry and ceder sour;
Bot cop and clapper, now is all ago.   (442)

'My cleir voice and courtly carrolling,
Whair I was wont with ladyis for to sing,
Is rauk as ruik, full hiddeous, hoir and hace;
My plesand port, all utheris precelling, bearing, surpassing
Of lustines I was hald maist conding;   excellent
Now is deformit the figour of my face;
To luik on it na leid now liking hes.
Soupit in syte, I say with sair sihing,   drowned, grief
Ludgeit amang the lipper leid, "Allace!"   folk

'O ladyis fair of Troy and Grece, attend   (452)
My misery, whilk nane may comprehend,

My frivoll fortoun, my infelicity,
My greit mischief, whilk na man can amend.
Be war in time, approchis neir the end,
And in your mind ane mirrour mak of me;
As I am now, peradventure that ye,
For all your miht, may cum to that same end,
Or ellis war, gif ony war may be.   worse

'Noht is your fairnes bot ane faiding flour,   (461)
Noht is your famous laud and hie honour   reputation
Bot wind inflat in uther mennis eiris;   puffed
Your roising reid to rotting sall retour.
Exempill mak of me in your memour,
Whilk of sic thingis wofull witnes beiris.
All welth in eird away as wind it weires;   well-being, passes
Be war thairfoir, approchis neir the hour;
Fortoun is fikkill when sho beginnis and steiris.'   (469)

Thus chidand with her drery desteny,
Weiping sho woik the niht fra end to end;
Bot all in vane; hir dule, hir cairfull cry,   sorrow
Miht not remeid, nor yit hir murning mend.   bring relief
Ane lipper lady rais and till hir wend,
And said, 'Why spurnis thou aganis the wall
To sla thyself and mend nathing at all?   (476)

'Sen thy weiping doubillis bot thy wo,
I counsall the mak vertew of ane neid;
To leir to clap thy clapper to and fro,
And leif efter the law of lipper leid.'
Thair was na buit, bot furth with thame sho yeid   remedy
Fra place to place, whill cauld and hounger sair
Compellit hir to be ane rank beggair.   (483)

That samin time, of Troy the garnisoun,   garrison
Whilk had to chiftane worthy Troilus,

Throu jeopardy of weir had strikken down
Knihtis of Grece in number marvellous;
With greit triumphe and laude victorious   refoicing
Agane to Troy riht royally they raid.
The way whair Cresseid with the lipper baid.   (490)

Seing that company come, all with ane stevin   voice
Thay gaif ane cry, and shuik coppis gude speid;
'Worthy lordis, for goddis lufe of hevin,
To us lipper part of your almous deid!'   alms-giving
Than to thair cry nobill Troilus tuik heid,
Having piety, neir by the place can pas
Whair Cresseid sat, not witting what sho was.   (497)

Than upon him sho kest up baith her ene,
And with ane blenk it come into his thoht
That he sumtime hir face befoir had sene.
Bot sho was in sic plie he knew hir noht;
Yit than hir luik into his mind it broht
The sweit visage and amorous blenking
Of fair Cresseid, sumtime his awin darling.   (504)

Na wonder was, suppois in mind that he
Tuik hir figure sa sone, and lo, now why:
The idole of ane thing in cace may be   image, by chance
Sa deip imprentit in the fantasy
That it deludis the wittis outwardly,
And sa appeiris in forme and like estait
Within the mind as it was figurait.   formed

Ane spark of lufe than till his hart culd spring,   (512)
And kendlit all his body in ane fire;
With hait fevir ane sweit and trimbling
Him tuik, whill he was reddy to expire;
To beir his sheild his breist began to tire;
Within ane while he changit mony hew,
And nevertheles not ane aneuther knew.   (518)

For knihtly piety and memoriall   compassion
Of fair Cresseid, ane girdill can he tak,
Ane purs of gold, and mony gay jouall,
And in the skirt of Cresseid down can swak;   fling
Than raid away, and not ane word he spak,
Pensive in hart, whill he come to the town,   (524)
And for greit cair oftsyis almaist fell down.   often

The lipper folk to Cresseid than can draw
To se the equall distribution
Of the almous; bot when the gold thay saw,
Ilk ane to uther prevely can roun,   whisper
And said, 'Yone lord hes mair affectioun,
However it be, unto yone lazarous
Than to us all; we knaw be his almous.'   (532)

'What lord is yone,' quod sho, 'have ye na feill, idea
Hes done to us so greit humanity?'
'Yes,' quod a lipper man, 'I knaw him weill;
Shir Troilus it is, gentill and fre.'   generous
When Cresseid understude that it was he,
Stiffer than steill thair stert ane bitter stound pang
Throuout hir hart, and fell doun to the ground. (539)

When sho ovircome, with sihing sair and sad,   revived
With mony cairfull cry and cald: 'Ochane!
Now is my breist with stormy stoundis stad,   beset
Wrappit in wo, ane wretch full will of wane!' devoid, hope
Than swounit sho full oft or sho wolde fane   stop
And ever in hir swouning cryit sho thus:
'O fals Cresseid and trew kniht Troilus!   (546)

'Thy lufe, thy lawty, and thy gentilnes   fidelity
I countit small in my prosperity,
Sa elevait I was in wantones,
And clam upon the fickill wheill sa hie.
All faith and lufe I promissit to the

43

Was in the self fickill and frivolous: itself
O fals Cresseid and trew kniht Troilus!   (553)

'For lufe of me thou keipt gude continence,   self-restraint
Honest and chaist in conversatioun;
Of all wemen protectour and defence
Thou was, and helpit thair opinioun.   reputation
My mind in fleschely foull affectioun
Was inclynit to lustis lecherous:
Fie fals Cresseid; O trew kniht Troilus!   (560)

'Lovers be war and tak gude heid about
Whome that ye lufe, for whome ye suffer paine.
I lat you wit, thair is riht few thairout
Whome ye may traist to have trew lufe agane;   in return
Preif when ye will, your labour is in vaine.   try
Thairfoir I reid ye tak thame as ye find,
For thay ar sad as widdercock in wind.   steadfast

'Becaus I knaw the greit unstabilnes,   (568)
Brukkill as glas, into myself, I say—
Traisting in uther als greit unfaithfulnes,   expecting
Als unconstant, and als untrew of fay—
Thoht sum be trew, I wait riht few ar thay;
Wha findis treuth, lat him his lady ruse;   extol
Nane but myself as now I will accuse.'   (574)

When this was said, with paper sho sat down,
And on this maneir maid hir testament:
'Heir I beteiche my corps and carioun   bequeath
With wormis and with taidis to be rent;
My cop and clapper, and mine ornament,
And all my gold the lipper folk sall have,
When I am deid, to bury me in grave.   (581)

'This royall ring, set with this ruby reid,
Whilk Troilus in drourie to me send,   as a love-token

44

To him agane I leif it when I am deid,
To mak my cairfull deid unto him kend.
Thus I conclude shortly, and mak ane end:
My spreit I leif to Diane, whair sho dwellis,
To walk with hir in waist woddis and wellis.   (588)

'O Diomeid, thou hes baith broche and belt
Whilk Troilus gave me in takning
Of his trew lufe'—and with that word sho swelt.   died
And sone ane lipper tuik of the ring,
Sine buryit hir withouttin tarying;
To Troilus furthwith the ring he bair,
And of Cresseid the deith he can declair.   (595)

When he had hard hir greit infirmity,
Hir legacy and lamentatioun,
And how sho endit in sic poverty,
He swelt for wo and fell doun in ane swoun;
For greit sorrow his hart to brist was boun;   burst
Sihing full sadly, said, 'I can no moir;
Sho was untrew, and wo is me thairfoir.'   (602)

Sum said he maid ane tomb of merbell gray,
And wrait hir name and superscriptioun,
And laid it on hir grave whair that sho lay,
In goldin letteris, conteining this ressoun:
'Lo, fair ladyis, Cresseid of Troyis town,
Sumtime countit the flour of womanheid,
Under this stane, lait lipper, lyis deid.'   (609)

Now, worthy wemen, in this ballet short,
Made for your worschip and instructioun,
Of cherity, I monishe and exhort,
Ming not your lufe with fals deceptioun;   mingle
Beir in your mind this short conclusioun   untimely end
Of fair Cresseid, as I have said befoir.
Sen sho is deid, I speik of hir no moir.   (616)

THE MORALL FABILLIS OF ESOPE THE PHRYGIAN

The Prolog

Thoht feinyeit fabils of ald poetre
Be not al grunded upon truth, yit than
Thair polite termes of sweit rhetore
Riht plesand ar unto the eir of man;
And als the caus that thay first began
Wes to repreif the haill misleving   *wrong living*
Of man be figure of ane uther thing.   (7)

In like maner as throu the bustious eird,   *rough earth*
Swa it be laubourit with grit diligence,
Springis the flouris and the corne abreird,   *sprouting*
Hailsum and gude to mannis sustenence,
Sa dois spring ane morall sweit sentence   *lesson*
Oute of the subtell dite of poetry,   *rhetoric*
To gude purpois wha culd it weill apply.   (14)

The nuttes shell, thoht it be hard and teuh,
Haldis the kirnill and is delectabill.
Sa lyis thair ane doctrine wise aneuh,
And full of fruit under ane fenyeit fabill;
And clerkis sayis it is riht profitabill
Amangis ernist to ming ane mery sport,
To light the spreit, and gar the time be short.   (21)

Forthermair, ane bow that is ay bent
Worthis unsmart and dullis on the string;   *weak, slackens*
Sa dois the mind that is ay diligent
In ernistfull thohtis and in studying;
With sad materis sum merines to ming,
Accordis weill: thus Esope said I wis,
'*Dulcius arrident seria picta Iocis*'   (28)

Of this authour, my maisteris, with your leif,
Submitting me in your correctioun,
In mother-toung of Lating I wald preif   *try*
To mak ane maner of translatioun;
Noht of myself, for vane presumptioun,
Bot be requiest and precept of ane lord,
Of whome the name it neidis not record.   (35)

In hamely language and in termes rude
Me neidis write, forwhy of eloquence   *because*
Nor rethorike I never understude.
Thairfoir meikly I pray your reverence,
Gif that ye find it throu my negligence
Be deminute, or yit superfluous,   *defective*
Correct it at your willis gratious.   (42)

My author in his fabillis tellis how
That brutal beistis spak, and understude
Into gude purpois dispute and argow,
Ane syllogisme propone, and eik conclude;
Put in exempill and similitude   *showing*
How mony men in operatioun
Ar like to beistis in conditioun.   (49)

Na mervell is ane man be like ane beist,
Whilk lufis ay carnall and foull delite;
That shame can not him renye nor arreist,   *govern*
Bot takis all the lust and appetite,
And that throu custum, and dayly rite;
Sine in thair mindis sa fast is radicate   *rooted*
That thay in brutal beistis ar transformate.   (56)

This nobill clerk Esope, as I haif tauld,
In gay metir, as poete lauriate,
Be figure wrait his buke; for he noht wald   *in figurative terms*
Lak the disdane of hie nor low estate.   *disparage*
And to begin, first of ane cok he wrate,

Seikand his meit, whilk fand ane joly stone,
Of whome the fabill ye sall heir anone. (63)

The Tail of the Cok and the Jasp

Ane cok, sum time, with feddram fresh and gay,
Riht cant and crous, albeit he was bot pure,   lusty, cocky
Flew furth upon ane dunghill sone be day;
To get his dennar set was al his cure.
Scraipand amang the as, be aventure   dirt
He fand ane joly jasp, riht precious,   jewel
Wes castin furth in sweping of the hous.   (70)

As damisellis wantoun and insolent,
That fane wald play, and on the streit be sene,
To swoping of the hous thay tak na tent;
Thay cair nathing, swa that the flure be clene.   care
Jouellis ar tint, as oftimis hes bene sene,   lost
Upon the flure, and swopit furth anone—
Peradventure sa wes the samin stone.   (77)

Sa mervelland upon the stane, quod he:
'O gentill jasp! O riche and nobill thing!
Thoht I the find, thou ganis not for me.
Thou art ane jowell for ane lord or king;
Piety it wer thou suld lie in this midding,
Be buryit thus amang this muke on mold,
And thou so fair and worth sa mekill gold.   (84)

'It is piety I suld the find, forwhy
Thy grit vertew, nor yit thy cullour cleir,
It may me nouther extoll nor magnify;
And thou to me may mak bot littill cheir.
To grit lordis thoht thou be leif and deir,   precious
I lufe fer better thing of les availl,   value
As draf or corne, to fill my tume intraill.   mash, empty

'I had lever haif scrapit heir with my naillis   (92)
Amangis this mow, and luke my lifis fude,   straw
As draf or corne, small wormis or snaillis,
Or ony meit wald do my stomok gude,
Than of jaspis ane mekill multitude;
And thou agane, upon the samin wyis,
For les availl may me as now dispyis.   (98)

'Thou hes na corne, and thairof haif I neid;
Thy cullour dois bot confort to the siht,
And that is not aneuh my wame to feid;
For wifis sayis lukand werkis ar liht.   outward shows are easy
I wald have sum meit, get it geve I miht,
For houngry men may not leve on lukis;
Had I dry breid, I compt not for na cukis.   (105)

'Whar suld thou mak thy habitatioun?
Whar suld thou dwell, bot in ane royall tour?
Whar suld thou sit, bot on ane kingis crown,
Exaltit in worship and in grit honour?
Rise, gentill jasp, of all stanis the flour,
Out of this midding, and pas whar thou suld be;
Thou ganis not for me, nor I for the.'   (112)

Levand this jowell law upon the ground,
To seik his meit this cok his wayis went.
Bot when or how or whome be it wes found,
As now I set to hald na argument.
Bot of the inward sentence and intent
Of this, as mine author dois write,
I sall reheirs in rude and hamely dite.   (119)

Moralitas
This joly jasp had properteis sevin:
The first, of cullour it was mervelous,
Part like the fire and part like to the hevin.
It makis ane man stark and victorious,   bold

49

Preservis als fra cacis perrillous.   circumstances
Wha hes this stane, sall have gude hap to speid,
Or fire nor water him neidis not to dreid.   (126)

This gentill jasp, riht different of hew,   distinctive
Betakinnis perfite prudence and cunning,
Ornate with mony deidis of vertew,   endowed
Mair excellent than ony eirthly thing;
Whilk makis men in honour for to ring,   reign
Happy, and stark to win the victory
Of all vicis and spirituall enemy.   (133)

Wha may be hardy, riche, and gratious?
Wha can eschew perrell and aventure?
Wha can governe ane realme, ciety or hous,
Without science? No man, I you assure.
It is riches that ever sall indure,
Whilk maith, nor moist, nor uther rust can freit;   moth, destroy
To mannis saull it is eternall meit.   (140)

This cok, desirand mair the sempill corne
Than ony jasp, may till ane fule be peir,
Whilk at science makis bot ane moik and scorne,
And na gude can; als littill will he leir.   learn
His hart wammillis wise argument to heir,   grows sick
As dois ane sow, to whome men for the nanis,
In hir draf-troih wald saw precious stanis.   swill-trough

Wha is enemy to science and cunning,   (148)
Bot ignorants that understandis noht?
Whilk is sa nobill, sa precious and sa ding,   worthy
That it may not with eirdly thing be boht?
Weill wer that man over all uther that moht
All his life-dayis in perfite study wair   spend
To get science; for him neidis na mair.   (154)

Bot now, allace, this jasp is tint and hid;
We seik it noht, nor preis it for to find.   strive

Haif we richis, na better life we bid,
Of science thoht the saull be bair and blind.
Of this mater to speik, it wer bot wind;
Thairfore I ceis and will na forther say.
Ga seik the jasp wha will, for thair it lay.   (161)

The Taill of the Uponlandis Mous and the Burges Mous

Esope, mine authour, makis mentioun
Of twa myis, and thay wer sisteris deir,
Of wham the eldest dwelt in ane borous-toun,
The uther winnit uponland weill neir,   lived in the country
Soliter, while under busk, while under breir,
Whilis in the corne, and uther mennis skaith,   harm
As outlawis dois and levis on their waith.   hunting

This rurall mous into the winter-tide,   (169)
Had hunger, cauld, and tholit grit distress;
The uther mous, that in the burgh can bide,
Was gild-brother and made ane fre burges;
Toll-fre als, but custom mair or les,   tax
And fredome had to ga whairever sho list,
Amang the cheis in ark, and meill in kist.   store

Ane time when sho was full and unfutesair,   (176)
Sho tuke in mind hir sister uponland,
And langit for to heir of hir weilfair,
To se what life sho had under the wand.   bough
Bairfute, allone, with pikestaf in hir hand,
As pure pilgrime sho passit out of town,
To seik her sister baith oure daill and down.   (182)

Furth mony wilsum wayis can sho walk,
Throu mosse and mure, throu bankis, busk and breir,
Sho ran criand whill she came to a balk: unploughed strip in
'Cum furth to me, my awin sister deir;   [ploughland

51

Cry peip anis!' With that the mous culd heir,
And knew hir voce as kinnisman will do,
Be verray kind; and furth sho come hir to.   instinct

The hartly joy, God geve ye had sene   (190)
Beis kith when that thir sisteris met!   shown
And grit kindnes wes shawin thame betwene,
For whilis thay leuh, and whilis for joy thay gret,
Whiles kissit sweit, whilis in armis plet;
And thus thay fure whill soberit wes thair mude,   (195)
Sine fute for fute unto the chalmer yude.   went

As I hard say, it was ane sober wane,   dwelling
Of fog and farne full febily wes maid,   moss, fern
Ane silly sheill under ane steidfast stane,   simple hovel
Of whilk the entres wes not hie nor braid.
And in the samin thay went but mair abaid,
Without fire or candill birnand briht,
For comonly sic pikeris lufis not liht.   pilferers

When thay wer lugit thus, thir sely mise,   (204)
The youngest sister into hir buttery glide,
And broht furth nuttis and candill insteid of spice;
Gif this wes gude fair, I do it on thame beside.   leave
The burges-mous prompit forth in pride,   burst out
And said, 'Sister, is this your daily fude?'
'Why not', quod sho,'is not this meit riht gude?'   (210)

'Na, be my saull, I think it bot ane scorne.'
'Madame,' quod sho, 'ye be the mair to blame.
My mother said, sister, when we wer borne,
That I and ye lay baith within ane wame;
I keip the rate and custome of my dame,   usage
And of my leving into poverty,
For landis have we nane in property.'   (217)

'My fair sister,' quod sho, 'have me excusit.
This rude diat and I can not accord;

To tender meit my stomok is ay usit,
For whilis I fair als weill as ony lord.
Thir widderit peis and nuttis, or thay be bord,   gnawed
Wil brek my teith, and mak my wame ful sklender,
Whilk wes before usit to meitis tender.'   (224)

'Weil, weil, sister,' quod the rurall mous,
'Geve it pleis you, sic thing as ye se heir,
Baith meit and dreink, harbery and hous,
Sal be your awin, will ye remane al yeir.
Ye sall it have with blyith and mery cheir,
And that suld mak the maissis that ar rude,   foods
Amang freindis, riht tender and wonder gude.   (231)

'What plesure is in the feistis delicate,
The whilkis ar gevin with ane glowmand brow?
Ane gentill hart is better recreate
With blyith curage, than seith to him ane kow;   cook
Ane modicum is mair for till allow,
Swa that gude will be kerver at the dais,   table
Than thrawin vult and mony spicit mais.'   ill-tempered air

For all hir mery exhortatioun,   (239)
This burges-mous had littill will to sing.
Bot hevily sho kest hir browis down,
For all the dainteis that sho culd hir bring.
Yit at the last sho said, half in hething,   derision
'Sister, this victuall and your royall feist,
May weill suffice unto ane rurall beist.   (245)

'Lat be this hole, and cum into my place;
I sall to you shaw be experience
My Gude Friday is better nor your Pace;   Easter
My dishe-likingis is worth your haill expence.
I have housis anew of grit defence;
Of cat, nor fall-trap, I have na dreid.'
'I grant,' quod sho; and on togidder thay yeid.   (252)

53

In stubbil array throu gers and corne,   awkward fashion,
And under buskis prevely couth thay creip;   [grass
The eldest wes the gyde and went beforne,
The younger to hir wayis tuke gude keip.
On niht thay ran, and on the day can sleip,
Whill in the morning, or the laverok sang,   lark
Thay fand the town, and in blithly couth gang.   (259)

Not fer fra thyne unto ane worthy wane,
This burges broht thame sone whare thay suld be.
Without 'God speid' thair herbery wes tane,
Into ane spence with vittell grit plenty;   larder
Baith cheis and butter upon thair skelfis hie,
And fleshe and fishe aneuh, baith freshe and salt,
And sekkis full of meill and eik of malt.   (266)

Eftir when thay disposit wer to dine,
Withoutin grace thay weshe and went to meit,
With all coursis that cukis culd devine,
Muttoun and beif, strikin in tailyeis greit.   cut, portions
Ane lordis fair thus couth thay counterfeit,
Except ane thing, thay drank the watter cleir
Insteid of wine; bot yit thay maid gude cheir.   (273)

With blyith upcast and mery countenance,
The eldest sister sperit at hir gest
Gif that sho be ressone fand difference
Betwix that chalmer and hir sary nest.
'Ye, dame,' quod sho, 'how lang will this lest?'
'For evermair, I wait, and langer to.'   know
'Gif it be swa, ye ar at eis,' quod sho.   (280)

Till eik thair cheir ane subcharge furth sho broht,   add to,
Ane plait of grottis, and ane dishe full of meill;   [side-dish
Thraf-cakkis als I trow sho spairit noht
Aboundantly about hir for to deill.
And mane full fine sho broht insteid of geill,   simmel-cake, jelly

54

And ane white candill out of ane coffer stall,   stole
Insteid of spice to gust thair mouth withall.   (287)

This maid thay mery whill thay miht na mair,
And 'Haill, Yule! Haill!' cryit upon hie;
Yit efter joy oftimes cummis cair,
And troubill efter grit prosperity.
Thus as thay sat in all thair jolity,
The spenser come with keyis in his hand,   steward
Oppinnit the dure, and thame at denner fand.   (294)

Thay taryit not to weshe, as I suppose,
Bot on to ga wha that miht formest win.
The burges had ane hole, and in sho gois;
Hir sister had na hole to hide hir in:
To se that sely mous it wes grit sin,
So desolate and will of ane gude reid;   devoid, plan
For verray dreid sho fell in swoun neir deid.   (301)

Bot as God wald, it fell ane happy cace;
The spenser had na laser for to bide,
Nouther to seik nor serche, to sker nor chace,
Bot on he went, and left the dure up wide.
The bald burges his passing weill hes spide;
Out of hir hole sho come, and cryit on hie:
'How fair ye, sister? Cry peip, whairever ye be.'   (308)

This rurall mous lay flatling on the ground,
And for the deith sho wes full sair dredand,
For till hir hart straik mony wofull stound;   struck, pang
As in ane fever sho trimbillit fute and hand.
And whan her sister in sic ply hir fand,
For verray piety sho began to greit,
Sine confort hir with wordis hunny-sweit.   (315)

'Why lie ye thus? Rise up, my sister deir!
Cum to your meit; this perrell is overpast.'

The uther answerit hir with hevy cheir:
'I may not eit, sa sair I am agast;
I had lever thir fourty dayis fast,
With watter-caill, and to gnaw benis or peis,   thin soup
Than all your feist in this dreid and diseis.'   (322)

With fair trety yit sho gart hir uprise,
And to the burde thay went and togidder sat,
And scantly had thay drunkin anis or twise,
When in come Gib Hunter, our joly cat,
And bad 'God speid!' The burges up with that,
And till her hole sho went as fire on flint;
Bawdronis the uther be the bak hes hint.   the cat

Fra fute to fute he kest hir to and fra,   (330)
Whilis up, whilis doun, als cant as ony kid;   lively
Whilis wald he lat hir rin under the stra,
Whilis wald he wink, and play with hir buk-heid.   hide and seek
Thus to the sely mous grit pane he did,
Whill at the last, throu fortune and gude hap,
Betwix ane burde and the wall sho crap.   (336)

And up in haist behind ane parraling   partition-wall
Sho clam so hie that Gilbert miht not get hir,
Sine be the cluke thair craftely can hing,   claws
Till he wes gane; hir cheir wes all the better.
Sine doun sho lap when thair wes nane to let hir,
And to the burges-mous loud can sho cry,   (342)
'Fairweill, sister, thy feist heir I defy!   renounce

'Thy mangery is mingit all with cair;   feast
Thy guse is gude, thy gansell sour as gall.   goose, sauce
The subcharge of thy service is bot sair,
Sa sall thou find heir efterwart na fall.
I thank yone courtine and yone perpall wall   partition-wall
Of my defence now fra yone crewall beist.
Almihty God, keip me fra sic ane feist!   (350)

56

'Wer I into the kith that I come fra,   place
For weill nor wo, suld I never cum agane.'
With that sho tuke her leif and furth can ga,
Whilis throu the corne, and whilis throu the plane;
When sho wes furth and fre sho wes full fane,
And merily markit unto the mure.   found her way
I can not tell how weill thairefter sho fure.   (357)

Bot I hard say sho passit to hir den,
Als warme as woll, suppose it wes not greit,
Full beinly stuffit, baith but and ben,   comfortably
Of beinis, and nuttis, peis, ry, and wheit.
Whenever sho list, sho had aneuh to eit,
In quiet and eis withoutin ony dreid;
Bot to hir sisteris feist na mair sho yeid.   (364)

Moralitas
Freindis, ye may find, and ye will tak heid,
Into this fabill ane gude morality.
As fitchis mingit ar with nobill seid,   vetches
Swa interminglit is adversity
With eirdly joy, swa that na estate is frie,
Without trubill and sum vexatioun;
And namely thay whilk climmis up maist hie,
That ar not content with small possessioun.   (372)

Blissed be sempill life withoutin dreid;
Blissed be sober feist in quiety;
Wha hes aneuh, of na mair hes he neid,
Thoht it be littill into quantaty.
Grit aboundance and blind prosperity
Oftimes makis ane evill conclusioun;
The sweitest life, thairfoir, in this cuntry,
Is sickernes with small possessioun.   security

O wanton man, that usis for to feid   (381)
Thy wambe, and makis it a God to be,

Luke to thy self! I warne the weill but dreid,
The cat cummis, and to the mous hes ee.
What vaillis than thy feist and royalty,
With dreidfull hart and tribulatioun?
Best thing in eird, thairfoir, I say for me,
Is blyithnes in hart, with small possessioun.   (388)

Thy awin fire, my friend, sa it be bot ane gleid,   ember
It warmis weill, and is worth gold to the.
And Solomon sayis, gif that thou will reid:
'Under the hevin thair can not better be
Than ay be blyith and leif in honesty.'
Whairfoir I may conclude be this ressoun:
Of eirthly joy it beiris maist degre,
Blyithnes in hart, with small possessioun.   (396)

The Taill of Shir Chantecleir and the Foxe

Thoht brutall beistis be irrationall,
That is to say, wantand discretioun,
Yit ilk ane in thair kind naturall
Hes mony divers inclinatioun.
The bair busteous, the wolf, the wilde lioun,
The fox fenyeit, crafty and cautelous,   cunning
The dog to bark on niht and keip the hous.   (403)

Sa different thay ar in properteis,
Unknawin to man, and sa infinite,
In kind havand sa fell diversiteis,   great
My cunning is excludit for to dite.
Forthy as now I purpose for to write
Ane cais I fand, whilk fell this ather yeir,   instance
Betwix ane foxe and ane gentill chantecleir.   (410)

Ane wedow dwelt, intill ane drop thay dayis,   village
Whilk wan hir fude of spinning on her rok,   distaff

58

And na mair had forsuth, as the fabill sayis,
Except of hennis sho had ane littill flok;
And thame to keip sho had ane joly cok,
Riht curageous, that to this wedow ay
Devidit niht, and crew befoir the day.   divided night from day

Ane littill fra this foirsaid wedowis hous,   (418)
Ane thorny shaw thair wes of grit defence,   thicket
Whairin ane foxe, crafty and cautelous,
Maid his repair, and dayly residence;
Whilk to this wedow did grit violence,
In piking of pultry baith day and niht,
And na way be revengit on him sho miht.   (424)

This wily tod, when that the lark couth sing,
Full sair hungry unto the town him drest,
Whair Chantecleir into the gray dawing,
Wery for niht, wes flowen fra his nest.
Lowrence this saw, and in his mind he kest
The jeperdy, the wayis, and the wile,
Be what menis he miht this cok begile.   (431)

Dissimuland into countenance and cheir,
On kneis fell, and simuland thus he said:
'Gude morne, my maister, gentill Chantecleir!'
With that the cok start bakwart in ane braid.   jerk
'Shir, be my saull, ye neid not be effraid,
Nor yit for me to start nor fle abak,
I come bot heir service to you to mak.   (438)

'Wald I not serve to you, it wer bot blame,
As I have done to your progenitouris;
Your father full oft fillit hes my wame,
And send me meit fra midding to the muris.   midden
And at his end I did my besy curis   efforts
To hald his heid, and gif him drinkis warme,
Sine at the last the sweit swelt in my arme.'   died

59

'Knew ye my father?' quod the cok and leuh.   (446)
'Yea, my fair sone, I held up his heid,
When that he deit under ane birkin beuh;   birchen
Sine said the Dirigie when that he wes deid.   dirge
Betwix us twa how suld thair be ane feid?   feud
Whame suld ye traist bot me, your servitour,
That to your father did sa grit honour?   (452)

'When I behald your fedderis fair and gent,
Your beik, your breist, your hekill, and your kame,
Shir, be my saull, and the Blissit Sacrament,
My hart is warme; me think I am at hame:
To mak you blyith, I wald creip on my wame,
In froist and snaw, in wedder wan and weit,
And lay my liart loikkis under your feit.'   grey

This fenyeit foxe, fals and dissimulate,   (460)
Maid to this cok ane cavillatioun: deceitful speech
'Ye ar, me think, changit and degenerate,
Fra your father of his conditioun;
Of crafty crawing he micht beir the crown,
For he wald on his tais stand and craw.
This wes na le; I stude beside and saw.'   (466)

With that the cok upon his tais hie,
Kest up his beik, and sang with all his miht.
Quod Shir Lowrence: 'Weill said, sa mot I the,   thrive
Ye ar your fatheris sone and air upriht.
Bot of his cunning yit ye want ane sliht.   knack
For' quod the tod, 'he wald, and haif na dout,
Baith wink, and craw, and turne him thryis about.'   (473)

The cok, infect with wind and fals vanegloir,
That mony puttis unto confusioun,
Traisting to win ane grit worship thairfoir,
Unwarly winkand, wawland up and down,   rolling his eyes
And sine to chant and craw he maid him boun.   ready

60

And suddandly, be he had crawin ane note,
The foxe wes war and hint him be the throte.   alert

Sine to the woid but tary with him hyit,   (481)
Of that crime haifand bot litill dout.
With that Pertok, Sprutok, and Toppok cryit;
The wedow hard, and with ane cry come out.
Seand the cace, sho sihit and gaif ane shout:
'How, murther, hay!' with ane hiddeous beir,   clamour
'Allace, now lost is gentill Chantecleir!'   (487)

As sho wer woid, with mony yell and cry,   mad
Rivand hir hair, upon hir breist can beit,
Sine, paill of hew, half in ane extasy,
Fell down for cair in swoning and in sweit.
With that the sely hennis left thair meit,
And, whill this wife wes lyand thus in swoun,
Fell in that cace in disputatioun.   (494)

'Allace', quod Pertok, makand sair murning,
With teiris grit attour hir cheikis fell;
'Yone wes our drourie, and our dayis darling,   sweetheart
Our nihtingall, and als our orloge bell,
Our walkrife watche, us for to warne and tell   vigilant
When that Aurora with hir curcheis gray,   kerchiefs
Put up hir heid betwix the niht and day.   (501)

'Wha sall our lemman be? Wha sall us leid?   lover
When we ar sad, wha sall unto us sing?
With his sweit bill he wald brek us the breid,
In all this warld wes thair ane kinder thing?
In paramouris he wald do us plesing,   love-making
At his power, as nature did him geif.
Now efter him, allace, how sall we leif?'   (508)

Quod Sprutok than, 'Ceis sister of your sorrow;
Ye be to mad for him sic murning mais:

61

We sall fair weill; I find, Sanct Johne to borrow,   be my witness
The proverb sayis, "Als gude lufe cummis as gais!"
I will put on my halidays clais,
And mak me fresh agane this joly May,
Sine chant this sang, "Wes never wedow sa gay!"   (515)

'He wes angry and held us ay in aw,
And woundit with the speir of jelousy.
Of chalmerglew, Pertok, full weill ye knaw,   love-making
Waistit he wes, of nature cauld and dry;
Sen he is gone, thairfoir, sister, say I,
Be blyith in baill, for that is best remeid: sorrow
Let quik to quik, and deid ga to the deid.'   (522)

Than Pertok spak, with feinyeit faith befoir:
'In lust but lufe he set all his delite;
Sister, ye wait, of sic as him ane scoir   without
Wald not suffice to slaik our appetite.
I heht be my hand, sen that he is quite,   gone
Within ane oulk, for shame and I durst speik,   week
To get ane berne suld better claw oure breik.'   man, bottom

Than Toppok like ane curate spak full crous: boldly
'Yone wes ane verray vengeance from the hevin;   (531)
He wes sa lous, and sa lecherous;
He had' quod scho 'kittokis ma than sevin.   trollops
Bot rihteous God, haldand the balandis evin,
Smitis riht sair, thoht He be patient,
For adultery, that will thame not repent.   (536)

'Pridefull he wes, and joyit of his sin,
And comptit not for Goddis favour nor feid,   enmity
Bot traistit ay to rax, and sa to rin,   prevail
Whill at the last his sinnis can him leid
To shamefull end, and to yone suddand deid.
Thairfoir it is the verray hand of God
That causit him be werryit with the tod.'   (543)

When this wes said, this wedow fra hir swoun
Start up on fute, and on hir kennettis criede,   little dogs
'How! Berk, Berry, Bawsy Broun,
Ripe Schaw, Rin Weil, Curtes, Nutty Clyde,
Togidder all but grunching furth ye glide!   without grumbling
Reskew my nobill cok, or he be slane,
Or ellis to me se ye cum never agane.'   (550)

With that, but baid, thay braidet over the bent;   bidding, bounded
As fire of flint thay over the feildis flaw;
Full wichtly thay throu wood and wateris went,   vigorously
And ceissit not Shir Lowrence whill thay saw.
Bot when he saw the kennettis cum on raw,
Unto the cok in mind he said, 'God sen
That I and thou wer fairly in my den.'   (557)

Then said the cok, with sum gude spirit inspirit,
'Do my counsall and I sall warrand the;
Hungry thou art, and for grit travell tirit,
Right faint of force, and may not ferther fle.
Swyith turne agane, and say that I and ye   quickly
Freindis ar maid, and fellowis for ane yeir;
Than will thay stint, I stand for it, and not steir.'   (564)

This tod, thoht he wes fals and frivolus,
And had fraudis his querrell to defend,   cause
Desavit wes be menis riht mervelous;
For falset failyeis ay at the latter end.
He start about, and cryit as he wes kend.
With that the cok he braid unto a beuh,   flew
Now juge ye all whairat Shir Lowrence leuh.   (571)

Begylit thus, the tod under the tre
On kneis fell, and said, 'Gude Chantecleir,
Cum doun agane, and I, but meit or fe,
Sal be your man and servand for ane yeir.'
'Na, fals theif and revar, stand not me neir.   robber

63

My bludy hekill, and my nek sa bla,
Hes partit freindship for ever betwene us twa.   (578)

'I wes unwise that winkit at thy will,
Whairthrou almaist I loissit had my heid.'
'I was mair fule', quod he, 'to be sa still,
Whairthrou to put my pray into pleid.'   jeopardy
'Fair on, fals theif, God keip me fra thy feid.'
With that the cok over the feildis tuke his fliht,   (584)
And in at the wedowis lever couth he liht.   louvre

  Moralitas

Now, worthy folk, suppose this be ane fabill,
And overheillit with typis figurall,   adorned, allegorical figures
Yit may ye find ane sentence riht agreabill,   meaning
Under thir fenyeit termis textuall·   deceitful
To our purpose this cok weill may we call
Nise proud men, void and vaneglorious.
Of kin and blude whilk ar presumpteous.   (592)

Fie, puft-up pride! Thou is full poisonabill!
Wha favoris the on force man haif ane fall.
Thy strenth is noht, thy stule standis unstabill;
Tak witnes of the feindis infernall,
Whilk houndit down wes fra that hevinly hall
To hellis hole, and to that hiddeous hous,
Because in pride thay wer presumpteous.   (599)

This fenyeit foxe may weill be figurate,   likened
To flatteraris with plesand wordis white,
With fals mening and mind maist toxicate,
To loif and le that settes thair haill delite.   flatter
All worthy folk at sic suld haif despite;
For whair is thair mair perrellous pestilence
Nor gif to learis haistely credence?   (606)

The wickit mind and adullatioun,
Of sucker sweit haifand the similitude,

Bitter as gall, and full of poisoun
To taist it is, wha cleirly understude.
Forthy, as now shortly to conclude,
Thir twa sinnis, flattery and vaneglore,
Ar vennomous; gude folk, fle thame thairfoir.   (613)

The Taill how this foirsaid Tod maid his Confessioun to
   Freir Wolf Waitskaith

Leif we this wedow glaid, I you assure,
Of Chantecleir mair blyith than I can tell,
And speik we of the subtell aventure
And desteny that to this foxe befell,
Whilk durst na mair with waitting intermell,   hunting
Als lang as leme or licht wes of the day,
Bot, bidand niht, full still lurkand he lay   (620)

Whill that Thetes the goddes of the flude
Phebus had callit to the harbery,   summoned as a guest
And Hesperous put up his cluddy hude,   cloudy
Shawand his lusty visage in the sky.
Than Lowrence luikit up, whair he couth ly,
And kest his hand upon his ee on hiht,
Mery and glade that cummit wes the niht.   (627)

Out of the wod unto ane hill he went,
Whair he miht se the twinkling sternis cleir,
And all the planetis of the firmament,
Thair cours and eik thair moving in the spheir,
Sum retrograde and sum stationeir,
And of the zodiak, in what degre
Thay wer ilk ane, as Lowrence leirnit me.   (634)

Than Saturne auld wes enterit in Capricorne,
And Juppiter movit in Sagittary,
And Mars up in the Rammis heid wes borne,

And Phebus in the Lioun furth can cary;
Venus the Crab, the Mone wes in Aquary;
Mercurius, the god of eloquence,
Into the Virgin maid his residence.   (641)

But astrolab, quadrant or almanak,
Teichit of nature be instructioun,
The moving of the hevin this tod can tak,
What influence and constellatioun
Wes like to fall upon the eirth adown;
And to himself he said, withoutin mair,   (647)
'Weill worth my father, that send me to the lair!   a blessing on,
                                                      [learning
'My desteny and eik my weird I ken,   fate
My aventure is cleirly to me kend;   destiny
With mischeif mingit is my mortall men,   lot
My misleving the soner bot gif I mend;
It is reward of sin ane shamefull end.
Thairfoir I will ga seik sum confessour,
And shryif me clene of my sinnis to this hour.   (655)

'Allace,' quod he, 'riht waryit ar we thevis!   cursed
Our lyifis set ilk niht in aventure;
Our cursit craft full mony man mischevis;
For ever we steill, and ever ar like pure.
In dreid and shame our dayis we indure;
Sine "Widdinek", and "Crakraip" callit als,
And till our hire hangit up be the hals.'   neck

Accusand thus his cankerit conscience,   (663)
Into ane craig he kest about his ee;
So saw he cummand ane littill than frome hence,
Ane worthy Doctor in Divinity,
Freir Wolf Waitskaith, in science wonder sle,   who lies in wait to do
To preich and pray wes new cummit fra the closter,   [harm
With beidis in hand, sayand his Pater Noster.   (669)

66

Seand this wolf, this wily tratour tod
On kneis fell, with hude into his nek.
'Welcome, my gostly father under God!'
Quod he, with mony binge and mony bek.   *cringe, bow*
'Ha!' quod the wolf, 'Shir Tod, for what effek
Mak ye sic feir? Rise up, put on your hude.'
'Father,' quod he, 'I haif grit cause to dude.   *do it*

'Ye ar mirrour, lanterne, and sicker way   (677)
Suld gyde sic sempill folk as me to grace.
Your bair feit, and your russet coull of gray,
Your lene cheik, your paill, pitious face,
Shawis to me your perfite halines;
For weill wer him, that anis in his live
Had hap to yow his sinnis for to schrive.'   (683)

'Na, sely Lowrence,' quod the wolf, and leuh;
'It plesis me that ye ar penitent.'
'Of reif and stouth, shir, I can tell aneuh;   *theft, robbery*
That causis me full sair for to repent.
Bot, father, bide still heir upon the bent,
I you beseik, and heir me to declair
My conscience that prikkis me sa sair.   (690)

'Weill,' quod the wolf, 'sit down upon thy kne.'
And he down bairheid sat full humilly
And sine began with 'Benedicity!'
When I this saw, I drew ane litill by,
For it effeiris nouther to heir, nor spy,   *is proper*
Nor to reveill thing said under that seill:
Unto the tod this-gait the wolf couth kneill.   (697)

'Art thou contrite, and sory in thy spreit   *soul*
For thy trespas?' 'Na, shir, I can not duid:
Me think that hennis ar sa hony-sweit,
And lambes fleshe that new ar lettin bluid;
For to repent my mind can not concluid

67

Bot of this thing, that I haif slane sa few.'
'Weill,' quod the wolf, 'in faith, thou art ane shrew.'   rogue

'Sen thou can not forthink thy wickitnes,   repent
Will thou forbeir in time to cum, and mend?'   (706)
'And I forbeir, how sall I leif, allace,
Haifand nane uther craft me to defend?
Neid causis me to steill whairevir I wend:
I eshame to thig; I can not wirk, ye wait;   beg
Yit wald I fane pretend to gentill stait.'   (711)

'Weill,' quod the wolf, thou wantis pointis twa
Belangand to perfite Confessioun.
To the thrid part of Penitence let us ga:
Will thou tak pane for thy transgressioun?'
'Na, shir, considder my complexioun,   constitution
Sely and waik, and of my nature tender;
Lo, will ye se, I am baith lene and sklender.'   (718)

'Yit, nevertheles, I wald, swa it wer liht,
Short, and not grevand to my tendernes,
Tak part of pane—fulfill it gif I miht—
To set my sely saull in way of grace.'
'Thou sall,' quod he, 'forbeir flesh untill Pasche,
To tame this corps, that cursit carioun;
And heir I reik the full remissioun.'   grant

'I grant thairto, swa ye will gif me leif   (726)
To eit puddingis, or laip ane littill blude,
Or heid, or feit, or paynches let me preif,   tripes, taste
In cace I fall no flesh into my fude.'   chance to get
'For grit mister I gif the leif to dude   necessity
Twise in the oulk, for neid may haif na law.'
'God yeild you, shir, for that text weill I knaw.'   (732)

When this wes said, the wolf his wayis went.
The foxe on fuit he fure unto the flude—

To fang him fish haillely wes his intent.
Bot when he saw the watter and wallis woude,   *wild waves*
Astonist all still into ane stair he stude
And said,'Better that I had biddin at hame,
Nor bene ane fishar in the devillis name.   (739)

'Now may I scraip my meit out of the sand,
And I haif nouther boittis, net nor bait.'
As he wes thus for falt of meit murnand,
Lukand about his leving for to lait,   *seek*
Under ane tre he saw ane trip of gait;   *herd of goats*
Than wes he blyith, and in ane heuh him hid,   *gully*
And fra the gait he stall ane litill kid.   (746)

Sine over the heuh unto the see he hyis,
And tuke the kid be the hornis twane,
And in the watter outher twyis or thryis
He doukit him, and till him can he sayne:
'Ga down, Shir Kid, cum up Shir Salmond agane!'
Whill he wes deid; sine to the land him drewh,
And of that new-maid salmond eit aneuh.   (753)

Thus finely fillit with young tender meit,
Unto ane derne for dreid he him addrest;   *hiding place*
Under ane busk, whair that the sone can beit,
To beik his breist and belly he thoht best;
And reklesly he said, whair he did rest,
Straikand his wame aganis the sonis heit,   *stroking, belly*
'Upon this wame set wer ane bolt full meit.'   *arrow*

When this wes said, the keipar of the gait,   (761)
Cairfull in hart his kid wes stollen away,
On everilk side full warly couth he wait,
Whill at the last he saw whair Lowrence lay.
Ane bow he bent, and flane with fedderis gray
He haillit to the heid, and, or he steird,
The foxe he prikkit fast unto the eird.   (767)

'Now,' quod the foxe, 'allace and wellaway!
Gorrit I am, and may na forther gang.   shot through
Me think na man may speik ane word in play,
Bot nowondayis in ernist it is tane.'
He harlit him, and out he drew his flane;   dragged
And for his kid, and uther violence,
He tuke his skin and maid ane recompence.   (774)

Moralitas
This suddand deith and unprovysit end
Of this fals tod, without provisioun,
Exempill is exhortand folk to amend,
For dreid of sic ane like confusioun;
For mony now hes gude professioun,
Yit not repentis nor for thair sinnis greit,
Because thay think thair lusty life sa sweit.   (781)

Sum bene also, throu consuetude and rite,   custom, habit
Vincust with carnall sensuality;
Suppose thay be as for the time contrite,
Can not forbeir, nor fra thair sinnis fle
Use drawis nature swa in property   dominates
Of beist and man, that neidlingis thay man do
As thay of lang time hes bene hantit to.   accustomed

Be war, gude folke, and feir this suddane shoit,   (789)
Whilk smitis sair withoutin resistence.
Attend wyisly, and in your hartis be noit;   be it noted
Aganis deith may na man mak defence.
Ceis of your sin, remord your conscience,   have remorse
Obey unto your God and ye sall wend,
Efter your deith, to blis withouttin end.   (795)

The Taill of the Sone and Air of the foirsaid Foxe, callit Father Wer;
alswa the Parliament of fourfuttit Beistis, haldin be the Lioun

This foirsaid foxe, that deit for his misdeid,
Had not ane barne wes gottin rihteously,
Till airschip be law that miht succeid,
Except ane sone, whilk in adultery
He gotten had in purches prively,   bastardy
And till his name wes callit Father War,
That luifit weill with pultry to tig and tar.   meddle and harass

It followis weill be ressoun naturall,   (803)
And gre be gre of riht comparisoun,
Of evill cummis war, of war cummis werst of all;   worse
Of wrangus geir cummis fals successioun.   evil stock
This foxe, bastard of generatioun,
Of verray kinde behuifit to be fals;
Swa wes his father and his grandshir als.   (809)

As nature will, seikand his meit be sent,
Of cace he fand his fatheris carioun,
Nakit, new slane; and till him hes he went,
Tuke up his heid, and on his kne fell down,
Thankand grit God of that conclusioun,
And said,'Now sall I bruke, sen I am air,   enjoy
The bounds whair thou wes wont for to repair.'   (816)

Fie ! Covetice, unkind and venemous!   unnatural
The sone wes fane he fand his father deid,
Be suddand shot, for deidis odious,
That he miht ringe and raxe intill his steid,   rule, have his way
Dreidand nathing the samin life to leid,
In thift and reif, as did his father befoir;
Bot to the end attent he tuke no moir.   (823)

Yit nevertheles, throu naturall piety,
The carioun upon his bak he tais.

'Now find I weill this proverb trew,' quod he,
'"Ay rinnis the foxe, als lang as he fute hais."'
Sine with the corps unto ane peit-poit gais,   bog-hole
Of watter full, and kest him in the deip,
And to the devill he gaif his banis to keip.   (830)

O fulishe man plungit in warldlines,
To conqueis warldly gude and gold and rent,
To put thy saull in pane or hevines,
To riche thy air, whilk efter thou art went,   heir
Have he thy gude, he takis bot small tent
To execute, to do, to satisfy
Thy letter will, thy det and legacy!   (837)

This tod, to rest him, he passit to ane craig,
And thair he hard ane busteous bugill blaw,
Whilk, as he thoht, maid all the warld to waig.   shake
Ane unicorne come lansand over ane law—
Than start he up, when he this hard and saw—
With horne in hand, ane bill in buste he bure;   box
Ane pursephant semely, I you assure.   (844)

Unto ane bank, whair he miht se about
On everilk side, in haist he culd him hy,
Shot out his voce full schill and gaif ane shout,
And on this wyis twise or thrise did cry.
With that the beistes in the feild thairby,
All mervelland what sic ane thing suld mene,
Gritly agast, thay gaderit on ane grene.   (851)

Out of ane bust ane bull sone can he braid,
And red the text withoutin tarying:
Commandand silence, sadly thus he said:
'The nobill lioun, of all beistis the king:
Greting to God, helth everlesting
To brutall beistis and irrationall
I send, as to my subjectis grit and small.   (858)

'My celsitude, and hie magnificence,   sovereign state
Lattis you to wait, that evin incontinent,   straightway
Thinkis the morne with royall deligence,
Upon this hill to hald ane parliament.
Straitly thairfoir I gif commandement
For to compeir befoir my tribunall,
Under all pane and perrell that may fall.'   (865)

The morrow come, and Phebus with his bemis
Consumit had the misty cluddis gray.
The ground wes grene, and als as gold it glemis
With gers growand gudely, grit and gay;
The spice thay spred to spring on everilk spray;
The lark, the maveis and the merll full hie,
Sweitly can sing, creippand fra tre to tre.   (872)

The leopardis come with crown of massy gold;
Beirand thay broht unto that hillis hiht,
With jaspis jonit, and royall rubeis rold,   interlinked
And mony diveris diamontis diht.
With towis proud ane palyeoun down thay piht;   ropes
And in that throne thair sat ane wild lioun,
In rob royall, with sceptour, swerd and crown.   (879)

Efter the tennour of the cry befoir,
That gais on all fourfuttit beistis in eird,
As thay commandit wer, withoutin moir,   more ado
Befoir thair lord the lioun thay appeird;
And what thay wer, to me as Lowrence leird,
I sall reheirs ane part of everilk kind,
Als fer as now occurris to my mind.   (886)

The Minotaur, ane monster mervelous;
Bellerophont that beist of bastardry;
The Warwolf, and the Pegase perillous,
Transformit be assent of sorcery;
The linx; the tiger full of tyrany;

73

The elephant, and eik the dromedary;
The cameill with his cran nek furth can cary.   long, advanced

The leopard, as I haif tauld beforne;   (894)
The anteloip with the sparth furth couth speid;   horn
The peyntit pantheir, and the unicorne;
The raindeir ran throu reveir, rone and reid;   thicket
The joly gillet, and the gentill steid;   mare
The asse, the mule, the hors of everilk kind;   (899)
The da, the ra, the hornit hart, the hind.   doe, roe-deer

The bull, the beir, the bugill and the bair,   wild ox, boar
The tame cat, wildcat and the wild wod-swine,
The hard-bakkit hurcheoun and the hirpland hair,
Baith otter and aip and pennit porcupine,
The gukit gait, the sely sheip, the swine,   stupid
The wild once, the buk, the welterand brok,   lynx
The foumart with the fibert furth can flok.   polecat, beaver

The gray grewhound with sleuthound furth can slide,   (908)
With doggis all divers and different;
The rattoun ran, the glebard furth can glide,   glow-worm
The whrinand whitret with the whasill went,   whining stoat
The feitho that hes furrit mony fent,   fitchew, hem
The mertrik, with the cunning and the con,   marten, rabbit, squirrel
The bow ran bane, and eik the lerioun.   cattle, swiftly, dormouse

The marmisset the mowdewart couth leid,   mole
Because that nature denyit had hir siht;   (916)
Thus dressit thay all furth for dreid of deid;
The musk; the litill mous with all hir miht   civet-cat
With haist sho haikit unto that hill of hiht;
And mony kind of beistis I couth not knaw   (920)
Befoir thair lord the lioun thay loutit law.   bowed

Seing thir beistis all at his bidding boun,   ready
He gaif ane braid, and luikit him about;   start

74

Than flatlingis to his feit thay fell all down,
For dried of deith thay droupit all in dout.
He lukit when that he saw thame lout,
And bad thame, with ane countenance full sweit:
'Be not efferit, bot stand up on your feit.   (928)

'I lat you wit my miht is merciabill,   harms
And steiris nane that ar to me prostrait;
Angry, austerne, and als unamiabill
To all that standfray ar to mine estait.   opposed
I rug, I reif all beistis that makis debait   rend, destroy
Aganis the miht of my magnificence;
Se nane pretend to pride in my presence.   (935)

'My celsitude and my hie majesty
With miht and mercy mingit sall be ay;
The lawest heir I can full sone up hie,
And mak him maister over you all I may.
The dromedary, gif he will mak deray,   disturbance
The grit camell, thoht he wer never sa crous,   bold
I can him law als litill as ane mous.   reduce

'Se neir be twenty milis whair I am   (943)
The kid sa saifly be the gaittis side,
The tod Lowry luke not to the lam,
Na revand beistis nouther rin nor ride.'
Thay couchit all efter that this wes cride;
The justice bad the court for to gar fence,   proclaim
The sutis callit, and foirfalt all absence.   fined

The panther, with his paintit coit-armour,   (950)
Fensit the court, as of the law effeird.
Than tod Lowry luikit whair he couth lour,   lurk
And start on fute, all stonist, and all steird;
Ryifand his hair, he cryit with ane reird,   tearing, loud voice
Quaikand for dreid and sihand couth he say:
'Allace this hour, allace this dulefull day!   (956)

75

'I wait this suddand sembly that I se,
Haifand the pointis of ane parliament,
Is maid to mar sic misdoars as me.
Thairfoir, geve I me shaw, I will be shent;   undone
I will be soht, and I be red absent;
To bide or fle it makis no remeid;
All is alike, thair followis not bot deid.'   (963)

Perplexit thus in his hart can he mene   ponder
Throu falset how he miht himself defend.
His hude he drew laih attour his ene,
And, winkand with ane eye, furth he wend;
Clinshand he come, that he miht not be kend,   limping
And, for dreddour that he suld bene arreist,   (969)
He playit bukhude behind, fra beist to beist.   hide-and-seek

O filit spreit, and cankerit conscience!   polluted
Befoir ane roy renyeit with rihteousnes,
Blakinnit cheikis and shamefull countenance!
Fairweill thy fame; now gone is all thy grace,
The phisnomy, the favour of thy face,
For thy defence is foull and diffigurate,   (976)
Broht to the liht, basit, blunt and blait.   timid, weak,
                                                                   [powerless

Be thou atteichit with thift or with tressoun,
For thy misdeid wrangous and wickit fay,   faith
Thy cheir changis, Lowrence; thou man luke down;
Thy worship of this warld is went away.
Luke to this tod, how he wes in effray,
And fle the filth of falset, I the reid,
Whairthrou thair followis sin and shamefull deid.   (984)

Compeirand thus befoir thair lord and king,
In ordour set as to thair estait effeird,
Of everilk kind he gart ane part furth bring,
And awfully he spak and at thame speird
Geve there wes ony kind of beistis in eird

76

Absent, and thairto gart thame deiply sweir;
And thay said: 'Nane, except ane stude gray meir.'   brood

'Ga, mak ane message sone unto that stude.'   (992)
The court than cryit: 'Now see, wha sall it be?'
'Cum furth, Lowry, lurkand under thy hude.'
'Na shir, mercy! Lo, I have bot ane ee;
Hurt in the hoche; cruikit as ye may se.   hind-leg
The wolf is better in ambassatry
And mair cunning in clergy fer than I.'   (998)

Rampand he said, 'Ga furth, bribouris baith!'   rearing up, rogues
And thay to ga withoutin tarying.
Over ron and rute thay ran togidder raith,   brushwood, undergrowth
And fand the meir at hir meit in the morning.
'Now,' quod the tod, 'Madame, cum to the king;
The court is callit and ye ar *Contumax*.'   guilty of contempt of
'Let be, Lowrence,' quod sho, 'your courtly knax.'   [court

'Maistres,' quod he, 'cum to the court ye mon;   (1006)
The lioun hes commandit so indeid.'
'Shir Tod, tak ye the flirdome and the fon;   stop, mockery,
I have respite ane yeir, and ye will reid.'   [nonsense
'I can not spell,' quod he, 'sa God me speid!
Heir is the wolf, ane nobill clerk at all,
And of this message is maid principall.   (1012)

'He is autentik and ane man of age,   qualified
And hes grit practik of the chanceliary;
Let him ga luke and reid your privilage,
And I sall stand and beir witnes you by.'
'Whair is thy respite?' quod the wolf, in hy.
'Shir, it is heir, under my hufe weill hid.'
'Hald up thy heill' quod he; and so sho did.   (1019)

Thoht he wes blindit with pride, yit he presumis
To luke down law whair that hir letter lay.

With that the meir gird him upon the gumis
And straik the hattrell of his heid away.   crown
Half out of lyif, thair lenand down he lay:
'Allace,' quod Lowrence, '*Lupus*, thou art loist!'
'His cunning,' quod the meir, 'wes worth sum coist!   (1026)

'Lowrence,' quod sho, 'will thou luke on my letter,
Sen that the wolf nathing thairof can win?'
'Na, be Sanct Bryde!' quod he, 'Me think it better
To sleip in haill nor in ane hurt skin.
Ane skrow I fand, and this wes writtin in—
For five shillingis I wald not anis forfaut him—
"*Felix quem faciunt aliena pericula cautum!*"   (1033)

With brokin skap and bludit cheikis reid,
This wretchit wolf weipand thus on he went,
Of his menye markand to get remeid;   injuries, intending
To tell the king the cace wes his intent.
'Shir,' quod the tod, 'bide still upon this bent   spot
And fra your browis weshe away the blude,
And tak ane drink, for it will do you gude.'   (1040)

To fetche watter this fraudfull fox furth fure;
Sidelingis abak he soht unto ane sike.   streamlet
On cace he meittis, cummand fra the mure,
Ane trip of lambis dansand on ane dyke.
This tratour tod, this tyrant and this tyke,
The fattest of this flock he fellit hais,
And eit his fill; sine to the wolf he gais.   (1047)

Thay drank togidder and sine thair journey takis;
Befoir the king sine kneillit on thair kne.
'Whair is yone meir, Shir Tod, wes *Contumax*?'
Than Lowrence said: 'My lord, speir not at me!
Speir at your Doctour of Divinity,
With his reid cap can tell you weill aneuh.'
With that the lioun and all the laif thay leuh.   (1054)

78

'Tell on the cais now, Lowrence; let us heir.'
'This witty wolf,' quod he, 'this clerk of age,
On your behalf he bad the meir compeir;
And sho allegit to ane privilage:
"Cum neir and se, and ye sall haif your wage!"
Because he red his rispite plane and weill,   exemption
Yone reid bonat sho rauht him with hir heill.'   (1061)

The lioun said, 'Be yone reid cap I ken
This taill is trew, wha tent unto it takis;
The greitest clerkis ar not the wisest men;
The hurt of ane happy the uther makis.'
As thay wer carpand in this cais, with knakis,   joking
And all the court in merines and in gam,
Swa come the yow, the mother of the lam.   (1068)

Befoir the justice on hir kneis fell,
Put out hir plaint on this wyis wofully:
'This harlet huresone and this hound of hell,
Devorit hes my lamb full doggitly,
Within ane mile, in contrair to your cry.
For Goddis lufe, my lord, gif me the law   (1074)
Of this lurker!' With that Lowrence let draw.   scoundrel, made to
                                                        [leave

'Bide!' quod the lioun. 'Limmer, let us se
Gif it be suthe the sely yow hes said.'
'Aa, soverane lord, saif your mercy!' quod he.
'My purpois wes with him for to haif plaid;
Causles he fled, as he had bene effraid;
For dreid of deith, he duschit over ane dyke
And brak his nek.' 'Thou leis,' quod sho, 'fals tyke!'   (1082)

'His deith be practik may be previt eith: evidence, easily
Thy gorry gumis and thy bludy snout,
The woll, the fleshe, yit stikkis on thy teith;
And that is evidence aneuh, but dout.'
The justice bad ga cheis ane assyis about;

And so thay did, and fand that he wes fals,
Of murther, thift, piking and tressoun als.   (1089)

Thay band him fast; the justice bad belyif
To gif the dome and tak of all his clais;
The wolf, that new-maid Doctour, couth him schrif.
Sine furth him led, and to the gallows gais,
And at the ledder-fute his leif he tais.
The aip was boucher, and bad him sone ascend, executioner
And hangit him; and thus he maid his end.   (1096)

 Moralitas
Riht as the minour in his minorall   metallurgical craft
Fair gold with fire may fra the leid weill win
Riht so under ane fabill figurall
Sad sentence man may seik, and efter fine— serious meaning
As dayly dois the Doctouris of Devine,
That to our leving full weill can apply
And paint thair mater furth be poetry.   (1103)

The lioun is the warld be liknes,
To whom loutis baith empriour and king,
And thinkis of this warld to get incres,
Thinkand dayly to get mair leving:
Sum for to reull, and sum to raxe and ring; dominate, rule
Sum gadderis geir, sum gold, sum uther gude;
To win this warld sum wirkis as thay wer wod. (1110)

The meir is men of gude conditioun,
As pilgrimes walkand in this wildernes,
Approvand that for riht religioun
Thair God only to pleis in everilk place;
Abstractit from this warldis wretchitnes,
Fehtand with lust, presumptioun and pride,
And fra this warld in mind ar mortifide.   (1117)

This wolf I likkin to sensuality,
As when, like brutall beistis, we accord

Our mind all to this warldis vanity,
Liking to tak and loif him as our lord:
Fle fast thairfra, gif thou will riht remord;   have remorse
Than sall ressoun rise, rax and ring,
And for thy saull thair is na better thing.   (1124)

Hir lufe I likkin to the thoht of deid.
Will thou remember, man, that thou man de?
Thou may brek sensuality's heid,
And fleshly lust away fra the sall fle,
Fra thou begin thy mind to mortify;
Salomonis saying thou may persaif heirin:
'Think on thy end, thou sall not glaidly sin.'   (1131)

This tod I likkin to temptationis,
Beirand to mind mony thohtis vane,
Assaultand men with sweit persuasionis,
Ay reddy for to trap thame in ane traine;   snare
Yit gif thay se sensuality neir slane,
And suddand deith draw neir with panis sore,
Thay go abak and temptis thame no moir.   (1138)

O Mediatour mercifull and meik,
Thou soveraigne Lord and King celestiall,
Thy celsitude maist humilly we beseik
Us to defend fra pane and perrellis all!
And help us up unto Thy hevinly hall,
In gloir whair we may se the face of God!
And thus endis the talking of the tod.   (1145)

The Preiching of the Swallow

The hie prudence, and wirking mervelous,
The profound wit of God omnipotent,
Is sa perfite and sa ingenious,
Excellent far all mannis jugement;

Forwhy to him all thing is ay present,
Riht as it is or ony time sall be,
Befoir the siht of his divinity.   (1152)

Thairfoir our saull with sensuality
So fetterit is in presoun corporall,
We may not cleirly understand nor se
God as he is nor thingis celestiall;
Our mirk and deidly corps naturall   evil, mortal
Blindis the spirituall operatioun,
Like as ane man wer bundin in presoun.   (1159)

In Metaphisik Aristotell sayis
That mannis saull is like ane bakkis ee   bat's
Whilk lurkis still als lang as liht of day is,
And in the gloming cummis furth to fle;
Hir ene ar waik, the sone sho may not se:
Sa is our saull with fantasy opprest
To knaw the thingis in nature manifest.   (1166)

For God is in his power infinite,
And mannis saull is febill and over-small,
Of understanding waik and unperfite,
To comprehend him that contenis all.
Nane suld presume be ressoun naturall
To seirche the secreitis of the Trinity,
Bot trow fermely and lat all ressoun be.   believe

Yit nevertheles we may haif knawlegeing   (1174)
Of God Almihty be his creatouris
That he is gude, fair, wyis and bening.
Exempill tak be thir joly flouris
Riht sweit of smell and plesant of colouris,
Sum grene, sum blew, sum purpour, white and reid,
Thus distribute be gift of his Godheid.   (1180)

The firmament paintit with sternis cleir,
From eist to west rolland in cirkill round,

And everilk planet in his proper spheir,
In moving makand harmony and sound;
The fire, the air, the watter, and the ground—
Till understand it is aneuh, I wis,
That God in all his werkis witty is.   wise

Luke weill the fishe that swimmis in the se;   (1188)
Luke weill in eirth all kind of bestiall;
The fowlis fair sa forcely thay fle,
Sheddand the air with pennis grit and small;
Sine luke to man, that he maid last of all,
Like to his image and his similitude:
Be thir we knaw that God is fair and gude.   (1194)

All creature he maid for the behufe
Of man, and to his supportatioun
Into this eirth, baith under and abufe,
In number, weht and dew proportioun;
The difference of time and ilk seasoun
Concorddand till our opurtunity,
As dayly by experience we may se.   (1201

The somer with his joly mantill of grene,
With flouris fair furrit on everilk fent,   trimmed
Whilk Flora goddes, of the flouris quene,
Hes to that lord as for his seasoun sent,
And Phebus with his goldin bemis gent
Hes purfellit and paintit plesandly   embroidered
With heit and moisture stilland from the sky.   distilling

Sine hervest hait, when Ceres that goddes   (1209)
Hir barnis benit hes with abundance;   filled
And Bachus, god of wine, renewit hes
The tume pyipis in Italy and France
With winis wiht, and liquour of plesance;   strong
And *Copia temporis* to fill hir horne,
That never wes full of wheit nor uther corne.   (1215)

83

Sine winter wan, when austerne Eolus,
God of the wind, with blastis boreall
The grene garment of somer glorious
Hes all to-rent and revin in pecis small;
Than flouris fair faidit with froist man fall,
And birdis blyith changit thair noitis sweit
In still murning, neir slane with snaw and sleit.   (1222)

Thir dalis deip with dubbis drownit is,   puddles
Baith hill and holt heillit with frostis hair;   hoar
And bewis bene laifit bair of blis   fair
Be wickit windis of the winter wair.
All wild beistis than from the bentis bair   fields
Drawis for dreid unto thair dennis deip,   (1228)
Coucheand for cauld in coifis thame to keip.   hollows, shelter

Sine cummis ver, when winter is away,   spring
The secretar of somer with his sell,   self
When columby up-keikis throu the clay,   peeps up
Whilk fleit wes befoir with froistes fell.
The mavis and the merle beginnis to mell;   mate
The lark on loft, with uther birdis haill,
Than drawis furth fra derne over down and daill.   hiding

That samin seasoun, into ane soft morning,   (1237)
Riht blith that bitter blastis wer ago,
Unto the wod, to se the flouris spring
And heir the mavis sing and birdis mo,
I passit furth, sine lukit to and fro
To se the soill that wes riht sessonabill,
Sappy and to resave all seidis abill.   (1243)

Moving thusgait, grit mirth I tuke in mind,
Of lauboraris to se the besines—
Sum makand dyke and sum the pleuh can wind,
Sum sawand seidis fast frome place to place,
The harrowis hoppand in the saweris trace:

84

It wes grit joy to him that luifit corne,
To se thame laubour baith at evin and morne.   (1250)

And as I baid under ane bank full bene,
In hart gritly rejosit of that siht,
Unto ane hedge, under ane hawthorne grene,
Of small birdis thair come ane ferly fliht,   sudden
And down belyif can on the leifis liht
On everilk side about me whair I stude,
Riht mervellous, ane mekill multitude.   (1257)

Amang the whilks ane swallow loud couth cry,
On that hawthorne hie in the croip sittand: tree-top
'O ye birdis on bewis heir me by,
Ye sall weill knaw and wisly understand
Whair danger is, or perrell appeirand;
It is grit wisedome to provide befoir,
It to devoid, for dreid it hurt you moir'.   shun

'Shir Swallow,' quod the lark agane and leuh,   (1265)
'What haif ye sene that causis you to dreid?'
'Se ye yone churll', quod sho, 'beyond yone pleuh   plowland
Fast sawand hemp and gude linget seid?   linseed
Yone lint will grow in litill time indeid,   flax
And thairof will yone churll his nettis mak,
Under the whilk he thinkis us to tak.   (1271)

'Thairfoir I reid we pas when he is gone,
At evin, and with our naillis sharp and small
Out of the eirth scraip we yone seid anone,
And eit it up; for gif it growis, we sall
Have cause to weip heirefter ane and all:
Se we remeid thairfoir furthwith instante,
Nam levius laedit quicquid praevidimus ante.   (1278)

'For clerkis sayis it is noht sufficient
To considder that is befoir thine ee;

Bot prudence is ane inwart argument
That garris ane man provide and foirse
What gude, what evill is likly for to be,
Of everilk thing behald the finall end
And swa fra perrell the better him defend.'   (1285)

The lark, lauhand, the swallow thus couth scorne,
And said sho fishit lang befoir the net;
'The barne is eith to busk that is unborne;   easy, swaddle
All growis noht that in the ground is set;
The nek to stoup, when it the straik sall get,
Is sone aneuh—deith on the fayest fall.'   doomed
Thus scornit thay the swallow ane and all.   (1292)

Despising thus hir helthsum document,   warning
The fowllis ferly tuke thair fliht anone;
Sum with ane bir thay braidit over the bent
And sum agane ar to the grene wod gone.
Upon the land whair I wes left allone,
I tuke my club and hamewart couth I cary,
Swa ferliand as I had sene ane fary.   amazed, vision

Thus passit furth whill June, that joly tide,   (1300)
And seidis that wer sawin of beforne
Wer growin hie, that hairis miht thame hide,
And als the quailye craikand in the corne;
I movit furth, betwix midday and morne,
Unto the hedge under the hawthorne grene
Whair I befoir the said birdis had sene.   (1306)

And as I stude, be aventure and cace,
The samin birdis as I haif said you air—
I hoip, because it wes thair hanting place,   accustomed
Mair of succour, or yit mair solitair—
Thay lihtit down; and, when thay lihtit wair,
The swallow swith put furth ane pietuous pime,   cry
Said, 'Wo is him can not bewar in time!   (1313)

'O blind birdis and full of negligence,
Unmindfull of your awin prosperity,
Lift up your siht, and tak gude advertence!
Luke to the lint that growis on yone le;
Yone is the thing I bad forsuith that we,
Whill it wes seid, suld rute furth of the eird:
Now is it lint; now is it hie on breird.   growth

'Go yit, whill it is tender and small,   (1321)
And pull it up; let it na mair incres.
My fleshe growis, my body quaikis all;   creeps
Thinkand on it I may not sleip in peis.'
Thay cryit all and bad the swallow ceis,
And said, 'Yone lint heirefter will do gude,
For linget is to litill birdis fude.   (1327)

'We think, when that yone lint-bollis ar ryip,
To mak us feist and fill us of the seid,
Magre yone churll, and on it sing and pyip.'   despite
'Weill,' quod the swallow, 'freindes, hardily beid;   by all means be
Do as ye will, bot certane sair I dreid,   [it so
Heirefter ye sall find als sour as sweit,
When ye ar speldit on yone carlis speit.   skewered

'The awner of yone lint ane fowler is,   (1335)
Riht cautelous and full of subtelty;
His pray full sendill-timis will he mis,   seldom
Bot gif we birdis all the warrer be;
Full mony of our kin he hes gart de,
And thoht it bot ane sport to spill thair blude:
God keip me fra him, and the Haly Rude.'   (1341)

Thir small birdis haveand bot litill thoht
Of perrell that miht fall be aventure,
The counsell of the swallow set at noht,
Bot tuke thair fliht, and furth togidder fure;
Sum to the wode, sum markit to the mure.   made for

I tuke my staff when this wes said and done,
And walkit hame, for it drew neir the none.   (1348)

The lint ryipit, the carll pullit the line,   stalks
Rippillit the bollis and in beitis set,   de-seeded, bundles
It steipit in the burne and dryit sine,
And with ane bittill knokkit it and bet,   beetle
Sine swingillit it weill and hekkillit in the flet;   scutched, combed,
His wife it span and twinit it into threid,   [indoors
Of whilk the fowlar nettis maid indeid.   (1355)

The winter come, the wickit wind can blaw,
The woddis grene were wallowit with the weit;
Baith firth and fell with froistis were maid faw,   bright
Slonkis and slaik maid sliddery with the sleit;   hollows, dells
The fowlis fair for falt thay fell of feit;   want
On bewis bair it wes na bute to bide,
Bot hyit unto housis thame to hide.   (1362)

Sum in the barn, sum in the stak of corne
Thair lugeing tuke and maid thair residence;
The fowlar saw, and grit aithis hes sworne
Thay suld be tane trewly for thair expence.
His nettis hes he set with diligence,
And in the snaw he shulit hes ane plane,   cleared, space
And heillit it all over with calf agane.   (1369)

Thir small birdis seand the calf wes glaid;
Trowand it had bene corne, thay lihtit down;
Bot of the nettis na presume thay had,   suspicion
Nor of the fowlaris fals intentioun;
To scraip, and seik thair meit thay maid thame boun.
The swallow on ane litill branche neir by,
Dreiddand for gyle, thus loud on thame couth cry: (1376)

'Into that calf scraip whill your naillis bleid;
Thair is na corne—ye laubour all in vane;

Trow ye yone churll for piety will you feid?
Na, na, he hes it heir layit for ane trane;
Remove, I reid, or ellis ye will be slane;
His nettis he hes set full prively,
Reddy to draw; in time be war forthy.'   therefor

Grit fule is he that puttis in dangeir   (1384)
His life, his honour, for ane thing of noht;
Grit fule is he that will not glaidly heir
Counsall in time, whill it availl him noht;
Grit fule is he that hes na thing in thoht
Bot thing present—and efter what may fall,
Nor of the end hes na memoriall.   (1390)

Thir small birdis for hunger famishit neir,
Full besy scraipand for to seik thair fude,
The counsall of the swallow wald not heir,
Suppois thair laubour did thame litill gude.
When sho thair fulishe hartis understude
Sa indurate, up in ane tre sho flew;
With that this churll over thame his nettis drew.   (1397)

Allace, it wes grit hartsair for to se
That bludy boucheour beit thay birdis down,
And for till heir, when thay wist weill to de,
Thair cairfull sang and lamentatioun!
Sum with ane staf he straik to eirth on swoun;
Of sum the heid he straik, of sum he brak the crag;   neck
Sum half on life he stoppit in his bag.   (1404)

And when the swallow saw that thay wer deid,
'Lo,' quod scho, 'thus is happinnis mony syis   times
On thame that will not tak counsall nor reid
Of prydent men or clerkis that ar wyis;
This grit perrell I tauld thame mair than thryis;
Now ar thay deid and wo is me thairfoir!'
Sho tuke hir fliht, bot I hir saw no moir.   (1411)

89

Moralitas

Lo, worthy folk, Esope that nobill clerk,
Ane poet worthy to be laureate,
When that he waikit from mair autentik werk,   was free, serious
With uther ma this foirsaid fabill wrate,
Whilk at this time may weill be applicate
To guid morall edificatioun,
Haifand ane sentence according to ressoun.   (1418)

This carll and bond of gentrice spoliate,   peasant, kindness,
Sawand this calf thir small birdis to sla,   [devoid
It is the feind, whilk fra the angelike state
Exylit is as fals apostata;
Whilk day and niht weryis not for to ga
Sawand poisoun in mony wickit thoht
In mannis saull, whilk Christ full deir hes boht.   (1425)

And when the saull as seid into the eird
Gevis consent unto delectioun,
The wickit thoht beginnis for to breird
In deidly sin, whilk is dampnatioun;
Ressoun is blindit with affectioun,
And carnall lust growis full grene and gay,
Throu consuetude hantit from day to day.   custom

Proceding furth be use and consuetude,   (1433)
The sin ryipis and shame is set onside;
The feind plettis his nettis sharp and rude,
And under plesance previly dois hide;
Sine on the feild he sawis calf full wide,
Whilk is bot tume and verray vanity
Of fleshly lust and vaine prosperity.   (1439)

Thir hungry birdis wretchis we may call,
As scraipand in this warldis vane plesance,
Greddy to gadder gudis temporall,
Whilk as the calf ar tume without substance,

Litill of availl and full of variance,
Like to the mow befoir the face of wind
Whiskis away and makis wretchis blind.   (1446)

This swallow, whilk eschaipit is the snair,
The haly preichour weill may signify,
Exhortand folk to walk and ay be wair
Fra nettis of our wickit enemy,
Wha sleipis not, bot ever is reddy,
When wretchis in this warld calf dois scraip,
To draw his net that thay may not eschaip.   (1453)

Allace, what cair, what weiping is and wo
When saull and body departit ar in twane!
The body to the wormis keitching go,
The saull to fire, to everlestand pane.
What helpis than this calf, thir gudis vane,
When thou art put in Luceferis bag
And broht to hell and hangit be the crag?   (1460)

Thir hid nettis for to persave and se,
This sary calf wyisly to understand,
Best is bewar in maist prosperite,
For in this warld thair is na thing lestand;
Is na man wait how lang his stait will stand,
His life will lest, nor how that he sall end
Efter his deith, nor whidder he sall wend.   (1467)

Pray we thairfoir, whill we ar in this life,
For four thingis: the first, fra sin remufe;
The secund is fra all weir and strife;
The thrid is perfite cherity and lufe;
The feird thing is—and maist for oure behufe—
That is in blis with angellis to be fallow.   companion
And thus endis the preiching of the swallow.   (1474)

91

The nobillness and gret magnificence
Of prince or lord, wha list to magnify,   wishes
His gret ancestry and lineall discence
Suld first extoll and his genology,
So that his hart he miht incline tharby
The mor to vertew and to worthiness,
Herand reherss his eldaris gentilness.   (7)

It is contrar the lawis of natur
A gentill man to be degenerat,
Noht following of his progenitour
The worthy reule and the lordly estate;
A ryall reulre for to be rusticat   boorish
Is bot a monstour in comparisoun,   (13)
Had in dispite and foule derisioun.   held

I say this be the gret lordis of Grewe,   Greece
Whilkis set thar hart, for all thair hale corage,   perfect
Thar faderis steppis justly to persewe,
Eking the worshipe of thar hie linage;   increasing, honour
The ancient and sadwis men of age   sober
War tendouris to the younge and insolent,   guides
To mak thaim in all vertew excellent.   (21)

Like as a strand of watter or a spring   stream
Haldis the sapour of his fontale well,   flavour, source
So did in Grece ilk lord and worthy king,
Of forbearis thai tuke carage and smell,   mien, character
Amangis the whilkis of ane I think to tell;
But first his gentill generacioun
I sall reherss, with your correctioun.   (28)

Apon the montane of Elicounee,
The most famouss of all Arabia,
A goddes dwelt, excellent of beute,

92

Gentill of blude, callit Memoria;
Whilk Jubiter that god to wif can ta,
And carnaly hir knewe, whilk efter sine,
Apon a day, bair him fair douchteris nine.   (35)

The first in Grewe was callit Euterpe,
In our langage gud delictacioun;   delight
The secound maide named Melpomane,
As hony sweit in modulacioun;   music
Tersicor, whilk is gud instructioun
Of every thing, the thrid sister, I wiss,
Thus out of Grewe in Latine translat is.   (42)

Caliope, that madin mervalous,
The ferd sister, of all musik maistress,
And moder to the king Shir Orpheus,
Whilk throu his wif was efter king of Trace;
Cleo, the fift, that now is a goddess,
In Latine callit meditacioun,
Of every thing that has creacioun.   (49)

The sext lady was callit Herato,
Whilk drawis like to like in every thing;
The sevint lady was callit fair Pollymyo,
Whilk coude a thousand sangis swetly sing;
Thelia sine, whilk can our saulis bring
To profound wit and gret agilite,   acuteness
To understand and have capacite.   (56)

Urania, the nint and last of all,
In our langage, wha coud it wele expound,
Is callit armony celestiall,
Rejosing men with melody and sound.
Amang thir nine Caliope was crownd,
And maid a quene be mihty god Phebus,
Of whom he gat this prince Shir Orpheus.   (63)

No wounder is thoht he was fair and wise,
Gentill and full of liberalite,
His fader god, and his progenitris
A goddess, findar of all ermonye;
When he was borne sho set him on hir kne,
And gart him souke of hir twa palpis white
The sweit licour of all musik perfite.   (70)

When he was auld, sone to manhed he drewe,
Of statur large, and frely fair of face;
His noble fame so far it sprang and grewe,
Till at the last the mihty quene of Trace,
Excellent fair, haboundand in richess,
Ane message send unto this prince so ying,
Requirand him to wed hir and be king.   (77)

Erudices that lady had to name.
When that sho saw this prince so glorius,
Hir erand to propone she thoht no shame,   purpose, declare
With wordis sweit and blenkis amorous,
Said, 'Welcome, lord and luf, Shir Orpheus,
In this province ye sall be king and lord!'
Thai kissit sine, and thus war at accord.   (84)

Betwene Orpheus and fair Erudices,
Fra thai war weddit, on fra day to day,
The lowe of luf couth kendill and encres,   flame
With mirth, blithness, gret plesans, and gret play
Of wardly joye; allace, what sall we say?
Like till a flour that plesandly will spring,
Whilk fadis sone, and endis with murning.   (91)

I say this be Erudices the quene,
Whilk walkit furth intill a May morning,
And with a madin, in a medow grene,
To take the dewe and se the flouris spring;
Whar in a shawe, ner by this lady ying,   grove

94

A bustuos herd callit Aristius,
Kepand his bestis, lay under a buss.   (98)

And when he saw this lady solitar,
Barfute, with shankis whitar than the snaw,
Prikkit with lust, he thoht withoutin mar   more ado
Hir till oppress, and till hir can he draw.
Dredand for scaith she fled, when sho him saw;
And as sho ran, all bairfut, in ane buss
Sho trampit on a serpent vennomuss.   (105)

This cruell vennome was so penitrif,
As natur is of all mortall poisoun,
In pecis small this quenis hart couth rife,
And sho anone fell in a dedly swoun.
Seand this caiss, Proserpine maid hir boun,   ready
Whilk clepit is the goddes infernall,   called
And till hir court this gentill quene couth call.   (112)

And when sho vanist was and invisible,
Hir madin wepit with a wofull cheir,
Cryand with mony shout and voce terrible,
Till at the last Shir Orpheus couth heir,
And of hir cry the causs than can he speir.
Sho said, 'Allace! Erudices, your quene,
Is with the fary tane befor mine ene.'   (119)

This noble king inflammit all in ire,
And rampand as ane lioun ravenus,
With awfull luke and eyne glowand as fire,
Speris the maner, and the maid said thus:
'Sho trampit on a serpent vennomouss,
And fell in swoun; with that the quene of fary
Clauht hir up sone and furth with hir can cary.'   (126)

When sho had said, the king sihit full sore,
His hert ner birst for verray dule and wo;   sorrow

95

Half out of mind, he maid na tary more,
But tuke his harp and to the wod can go,
Wringand his handis, walkand to and fro,
Whill he miht stand, sine sat down on a stone,   (132)
And to his harp thusgate he maid his mone: *in this manner*

'O dulfull harp, with mony dolly string,   *mournfull*
Turne all thy mirth and musik in murning,
And cess of all thy subtell sangis sweit;
Now wepe with me, thy lord and carefull king,
Whilk losit has in erd all his liking;   *delight*
And all thy game thou change in gule and greit,   *howling, lamentation*
Thy goldin pinnis with thy teris weit,   *(harp) pegs*
And all my pane for to report thou press,   *strive*
Cryand with me in every steid and streit,
"Whar art thou gane, my luf Erudices?" '   (143)

Him to rejoss yit playit he a spring,
Whill all the fowlis of the wod can sing,
And treis dansit with thair leves grene,
Him to devoid of his gret womenting;   *sorrow*
Bot all in vane—thai comfort him nothing,
His hart was sa apon his lusty quene;
The bludy teres sprang out of his eyne,
Thar was na solace miht his sobbing cess,
Bot cryit ay, with caris cald and kene,
'Whar art thou gane, my luf Erudices?   (153)

'Fairweill my place, fairwele plesance and play,
And welcome woddis wild and wilsome way,   *wandering*
My wikit werd in wilderness to wair;   *fate, endure*
My rob ryall and all my riche array
Chaungit sall be in rude russat of gray,
My diademe intill ane hat of hair;
My bed sall be with bever, broke and bair,   *badger, boar*
In buskis bene with mony bustuoss bess,
Withoutin sang, saying with sihing sair,
"Whar art thou gane, my luf Erudices?"   (163)

'I the beseike, my fair fader Phebus,
Have pete of thy awne son Orpheus;
Wait thou noht wele I am thy barne and child?   know
Now heir my plant, panefull and petuouss;
Direct me fra this deid sa doloruss,
Whilk gois thus withoutin gilt begild;   cheated
Lat noht thy face with cloudis be oursild;   overcast
Len me thy liht, and lat me noht ga less,   without
To find the fair in fame that never was fild,   defiled
My lady quene and luf, Erudices.   (173)

'O Jupiter, thou god celestiall,
And grantshir to myself, on the I call
To mend my murning and my drery mone;
Thou gif me forss that I noht fant nor fall,
Whill I hir find; for seik hir suth I sall,   truly
And nother stint nor stand for stok nor stone.
Throu thy godhed gyde me whar sho is gone,
Gar hir appeir and put mine hert in pess.'
Thus King Orpheus, with his harpe allone,
Sore wepit for his wif Erudices.   (183)

When endit was the sangis lamentable,
He tuke his harp and on his brest can hing,
Sine passit to the hevin, as sayis the fable,
To seik his wif, bot that avalit nathing.
By Wadling Streit he went but tarying,
Sine come downe throu the speir of Saturn ald,   sphere
Whilk fader is of all thir sternis cald.   (190)

When sho was souht outthrou that cald regioun,
To Jubiter his grantshir can he wend,
Whilk rewit sair his lamentacioun,
And gart his speir be souht fra end to end;   searched
Sho was noht thare; than down he can discend
To Mars, the god of batall and of strif,
And soht his speir, yit gat he noht his wif.   (197)

97

Sine went he downe to his fader Phebus,
God of the son, with bemes briht and cleir;
When that he saw his sone Orpheus
In sic a plite, it changit all his cheir.
He gart anone go seik throu all his speir;
Bot all in vane, that lady come noht thare.
Than tuke he leif and to Venus can fair.   go

When he hir saw, he knelit and said thus: (205)
'Wait ye noht weil I am your awne trew kniht?
In luf nane lelar than Shir Orpheus;
And ye of luf goddess, and most of miht,
Of my lady helpe me to get a siht.'
'For suth,' quod sho, 'ye mon seik nethirmar.'   lower down
Than fra Venus he tuke his lef but mair.   more ado

To Marcury but tary is he gone,   (212)
Whilk callit is the god of eloquens;
Bot of his wif thare knawlege gat he none.
With wofull hart than passit he downe fro thens;
Unto the mone he maid no residens.
Thus fra the hevin he went down to the erd,
Yit be the way sum melody he lerd.   learnt

In his passage amang the planetis all,   (219)
He herd ane hevinly melody and sound,
Passing all instrumentis musicall,
Causit be rolling of the speris round;
Whilk ermony throu all this mapamond,   world
Whill moving cess unite perpetuall,   unison
Whilk of this warld Pluto the saull can call.   (225)

Thar leirit he tonis proporcionate,
As dupler, tripler, and emetricus,   duple, triple(time),
Enoleus, and eike the quadruplat,   [proportion
Epodyus riht hard and curiouss;
And of thir sex, swet and delicious,

98

Riht consonant five hevinly symphonyis
Componit ar, as clerkis can devis. (232)

First diatasseroun, full sweit, I wiss, interval of a fourth
And diapasoun, simple and duplate, interval of an octave
And diapente, componit with a diss; interval of a fifth
This makis five of thre multiplicat.
This mery musik and mellifluat,
Complete and full with noumeris od and evin,
Is causit be the moving of the hevin. (239)

Of sic musik to write I do bot dote,
Tharfor at this mater a stra I lay,
For in my lif I couth nevir sing a note;
Bot I will tell how Orpheus tuke the way,
To seike his wif attour the gravis gray, among, groves
Hungry and cald, our mony wilsom wane, over, wandering way
Withoutin gyde, he and his harp allane. (246)

He passit furth the space of twenty dayis,
Far and full ferther than I can tell,
And ay he fand stretis and redy wayis;
Till at the last unto the yet of hell
He come, and thare he fand a portare fell, fierce
With thre hedis, was callit Cerberus,
A hound of hell, a monstour mervalouss. (253)

Than Orpheus began to be agast,
When he beheld that ugly hellis hound;
He tuke his harpe and on it plait fast,
Till at the last, throu swetness of the sound,
The dog slepit and fell unto the ground;
And Orpheus attour his wame in stall, belly, stole
And nethirmar he went, as ye heir sall. (260)

Than come he till a river wounder depe,
Our it a brig, and on it sisteris thre, bridge

Whilk had the entre of the brig to kepe,
Alecto, Megera, and Thesphonee,
Tornand a wheile was ugly for to se,
And on it spred a man heht Ixioun,
Rollit about riht wounder wobegone.   (267)

Than Orpheus playit a joly spring,
The thre sisteris full fast thai fell on slepe,
The ugly wheile cessit of hir whirling;
Thus left was nane the entre for to kepe.
Than Ixioun out of the whele can crepe,
And stall away; than Orpheus anone,
Without stopping, attour the brig is gone.   (274)

Sine come he till a wounder grisly flude,
Droubly and depe, that rathly doun can rin,   turbid, swiftly
Whare Tantalus nakit full thristy stude,
And yit the wattir stud above his chin;
Thoht he gapit thar wald na drop cum in;
When he dulkit the wattir wald discend;   ducked
Thus gat he noht his thrist to slaike nor mend.   (281)

Before his face ane apill hang also,
Fast at his mouth apon a tolter threid;   swinging
When he gapit, it rokkit to and fro,
And fled, as it refusit him to feid.
Than Orpheus had reuth of his gret neid,   pity
Tuke out his harpe and fast on it can clink;
The wattir stude, and Tantalus gat a drink.   (288)

Sine our a mure, with thornis thik and sharp,
Weping allone, a wilsom way he went,
And had noht bene throu suffrage of his harp,   aid
With sharpe pikis he had bene shorn and shent;   injured
And as he blent, besid him on the bent   looked
He saw speldit a wounder wofull wiht,   stretched
Nalit full fast, and Tityus he hiht.   (295)

And on his brest thar sat ane grisly gripe,   vulture
Whilk with his bill his baly throu can bore,
Baith maw, midred, hart, lever, and tripe,   stomach, midriff
He ruggit out—his panis wer the more.   tore
When Orpheus saw him thus suffer sore,
Has tane his harpe and maid sweit melody—
The gripe is fled; Tityus left his cry.   (302)

Beyonde this mure he fand a ferefull strete,
Mirk as the niht, to pass riht dangerouss,
For slidderiness scant miht he hald his feit,
In whilk thar was ane stink riht odiouss,
That gydit him to hidouiss hellis houss,
Whar Rodomantus and Proserpina
War king and quene; Orpheus in can ga.   (309)

O dolly place, and groundless depe dungeoun!
Furness of fire, with stink intollerable,
Pit of dispair, without remissioun,
Thy meit vennom, thy drink is poisonable,
Thy gret panis to compt innomerable;
What creatur cummis to dwell in the
Is aye deand, and nevir more may de!   (316)

Thar fand he mony carefull king and quene,
With crowne on hed, of brass full hate birnand,
Whilk in thar lif riht masterfull had bene,
Conquerour of gold, richess, and of land.
Hector of Troye, and Priame, thar he fand;
And Alexander, for his wrang conquest;
Antiochus thar for his foule incest.   (323)

Thar fand he Julius Cesar for his cruelte;
And Herod with his brotheris wif he saw;
And Nero for his gret iniquite;
And Pilat for his breking of the law;
Sine efter that he lukit, and couth knawe

Cresus the king, non mihtiare on mold
For covatuss, yet full of birnand gold.   (330)

Thar fand he Pharo, for oppressioun
Of godis folk, on whilk the plagis fell;
And Saull eke, for the gret abusioun
Of justice to the folk of Israell;
Thar fand Acab and the quene Jesabell,
Whilk sely Nabot, that was a prophet trewe,
For his vine-yard withoutin pete slew.   (337)

Thar fand he mony pape and cardinal,
In haly kirk whilk dois abusioun,
And bischopis in thar pontificall,   episcopal vestments
Be simony for wrang ministracioun;
Abbotis and men of all religioun,
For evill disponing of thar placis rent,
In flam of fire war bittirly torment.   (344)

Sine nethirmar he went whar Pluto was,   lower down
And Proserpine, and thiddirwart he drewe,
Aye playand on his harpe as he couth pass;
Till at the last Erudices he knewe,
Lene and dedlike, petuoss and pale of hewe,
Richt warshe and wan, and wallowit as a weid,   pallid, withered
Hir lely lire was like unto the leid.   (351)

Quod he, 'My lady leil, and my delite,
Ful wa is me till se you changit thus;
Whar is thy rude as ross with cheikis white,   complexion
Thy cristall eyne with blenkis amoruss,
Thy lippis red to kiss deliciouss?'
Quod sho, 'As now I dar noht tell, perfaye;   truly
Bot ye sall wit the causs ane nothir day.'   (358)

Quod Pluto, 'Shir, thoht she be like ane elf,
Thar is na causs to plenye, and forwhy?   lament

Sho fare als wele daly as dois my self,
Or king Herod for all his chevalry.
It is langour that putis hir in sic ply;   state
War sho at home in hir cuntre of Trace,
Sho wald refet full sone in fax and face.'   revive, hair

Than Orpheus befor Pluto sat downe,   (366)
And in his handis white his harp can ta,
And playit mony sweit proporcioun,
With base tonis in Ipodorica,   Hypodorian mode
With gemining in Ipolirica;   variations, Hypolocrian mode
Til at the last for reuth and gret pete,
Thai wepit sore, that couth him heir or se.   (372)

Than Proserpine and Pluto bad him ass   ask
His warisoun; and he wald ask riht noht   reward
Bot licence with his wif away to pass
Till his countre, that he so fer had soht.
Quod Proserpine, 'Sen I hir hiddir broht,
We sall noht part bot with condicioun.'
Quod he, 'Tharto I mak promissioun.'   promise

'Erudices than be the hand thou tak,   (380)
And pass thy way, bot undirneth this pane;   penalty
Gif thou tornes or blenkis behind thi bak,
We sall hir have forevir till hell agane.'
Thoht this was hard, yit Orpheus was fane,   glad
And on thai went, talkand of play and sport,
Whill thai allmast come to the uttir port.   gate

Thus Orpheus, with inwart luf replet,   (387)
So blindit was in gret effectioun,
Pensif apon his wif and lady sweit,
Rememberit noht his hard condicioun.
What will ye more? in short conclusioun,
He blent bakwart, and Pluto come anone,   glanced
And unto hell agane with hir is gone.   (393)

Allace! It was riht gret hartsair to heir
Of Orpheus the weping and the wo,
When that his wif, whilk he had boht so deir,
Bot for a luke so sone was hint him fro.
Flatlingis he fell, and miht no forther go,
And lay a while in swoun and extasy;
When he ourcome, thus out of luf can cry: recovered

'What art thou, luf, how sall I the diffine?   (401)
Bitter and sweit, cruell and merciable,
Plesand to sum, till uthir plaint and pine,
Till sum constant, till uther variable.
Hard is thy law, thy bandis unbrekable;
Wha serviss the, thoht he be never so trewe,
Perchance sumtime he sall have caus to rew.   (407)

'Now find I weile, this proverb trewe' quod he,
"Hart is on the hurd, and hand is on the sore;   hoard
Whar luf gois, on forss tornes the ee".   of necessity
I am expert, and wo is me therfore;
Bot for a luke my lady is forlore.'   lost
Thus chidand on with luf, our burn and bent,
A wofull wedaw hamwart is he went.   (414)

  Moralitas
Lo, worthy folke, Boece, that senatur,
To write this faynit fable tuke in cure,
In his gay buke of consolacioun,
For our doctrine and gud instructioun;
Whilk in the self supposs it fenyeit be,
And hid under the cloke of poecy,   (420)
Yit master Trevit doctor Nicholass,
Whilk in his time a noble theologe was,
Applyis it to gud moralite,
Riht full of frut and seriosite.
Fair Phebus is the god of sapiens;   wisdom
Caliope, his wif, is eloquens;

104

Thai twa maryt gat Orpheus belif,   *straightway*
Whilk callit is the pairt intellectif
Of mannis saull, in undirstanding fre,
And separate fra sensualite.   (430)
Erudices is our effectioun,
Be fantasy oft movit up and down;
Whilis to resoun it castis the delite,
Whilis to the fleshe settis the appetite.
Aristius, this herd that couth persew
Erudices, is noht bot gud vertew,
Whilk besy is aye to kepe our mindis clene;
Bot when we fle outthro the medow grene
Fra vertew, to this warldis vane plesans,
Mengit with cair and full of varians,   (440)
The serpent stangis, that is dedly sin,
That poisonis the saule baith without and in;
And than is it deid, and eik oppressit down
To wardly lust all our effectioun.
Than perfite resoun wepis wounder sair,
Seand our appetit thusgate misfair;   *go astray*
And passis up to the hevin belif,
Shawand till us the lif contemplatif,
The parfit will, and alss the fervent luf
We suld have allway to the hevin abuf;   (450)
Bot seldin thar our appetit is fund,
It is so fast into the body bund;
Tharfor downwart we cast our mindis ee,
Blindit with lust, and may noht upwart fle;
Suld our desire be souht up in the speris,   *spheres*
When it is tedderit on this warldis breris, *caught up, briers*
While on the fleshe, while on this warldis wrak; *goods*
And to the hevin small entent we tak.   *heed*
Shir Orpheus, thou seikis all in vane
Thy wif so hie; therfor cum downe agane,   (460)
And pass unto yone monstour mervalus,
With thre hedis, that we call Cerberus,
Whilk feynit is to haf sa mony heidis,

For to betakin thre maner of deides.
The first is in the tendir young barnage, youth
The second deid is in the middle age,
The thrid is in gret eld when men ar tane.
Thus Cerberus to swelly sparis nane,
Bot when that ressoun and intelligens
Playis apon the harpe of eloquens; (470)
That is to saye, makis persuasioun
To draw our will and our affectioun,
In every eild, fra sin and foule delite, age
This dog our saull has na power to bite.
The secound monstouris ar the sisteris thre,
Alecto, Megera, and Thesiphonee,
Ar noht ellis, in bukis as we reid,
Bot wikit thoht, evill word, and frawerd deid. wayward
Alecto is the bolning of the hart, swelling
Megera is the wikit word outwart, expressed
Thesiphonee is operacioun (481)
That makis finale execucioun
Of dedly sin; and thir thre tornes aye
Ane uglye wheil, is noht ellis to say,
That wardly men sumtime ar cassin hie raised
Apon the whele, in gret prosperite,
And with a whirll, unwarly, or thai wait, without warning
Ar thrawin downe to pure and law estaite.
Of Ixioun that in the whele was spred,
I sall the tell sum part, as I have red; (490)
He was on lif broukle and lichoruss, frail
And in that craft hardy and coragiouss,
That he wald noht luf in na lawar place
Bot Juno, quene of natur and goddas.
And on a day he went up in the sky,
Sekand Juno, thinkand with hir to lie;
Sho saw him cum and knew his full entent.
Ane rany clud down fro the firmament
Sho gart discend, and kest betwene thaim two;
And in that clud his natur yeid him fro, semen

Of whilk was generit the Centauriss,   (501)
Half man, half horss, apon a ferly wiss.
Than for the inwart crabbing and offence   vexation
That Juno tuke for his gret violence,
Sho send him downe unto the sisteris thre,
Apon thar whele ay torned for to be.
Bot when that ressoun and intelligens
Plays apon the harp of consciens,
That is to say, the gret sollicitud,
While up, while down, to win this warldis gud,   (510)
Cessis furthwith, and our complexioun   nature
Waxis quiet in contemplacioun.
This Tantalus, of whom I spak of air,
Whill he levit he was a gay hostillar,   inn-keeper
And on a niht come travelland tharby
The god of riches, and tuke herbery
With Tantalus; and he to the supar
Slewe his awne sone, that was to him leif and deir,
Intill a sowe with spicis soddin wele,   broth, boiled
And gart the god eite up his fleshe ilk dele.   (520)
For this dispite, when he was deid anone,   offence
Was dampnit in the flude of Acheron,
To suffer hunger, thrist, nakit and cald,
Riht wo begone, as I tofore have tald.
This hungry man and thristy, Tantalus,
Betakinnis men gredy and covatuss,
The god of riches that is ay redy
For to resaif, and call in herbery;   as a guest
And to thaim seith thair sone in pecis small,
That is thair fleshe and blud, with gret travall,   (530)
To fill the bag, and nevir find in thair hert   amass wealth
Apon thaimself to spend, nor tak thair part.
Allace, in erd whar is thair mar foly,
Than for to want, and have haboundantly,
To have distress on bed, bak, and burd,
And spair till uther men of gold a hurde?
And in the niht slepe soundly may thai noht,

To gadder geir sa gredy is thair thoht.
Bot when that ressoun and intelligens
Playis apon the harp of eloquens,   (540)
That is to say, gettin with gret laubour,
Kepit with dreid, and tint is with dolour.
This avarice, be grace wha understud,
I trow suld leve thair gret sollicitud,
And ithand thohtis and thair besiness   busy
To gadder gold, and sine leif in distress;
Bot he suld drink ineuh whenevir him list
Of covatuss, and slaik the birnand thrist.
This Tityus lay nalit on the bent,
And with the gripe his bowallis revin and rent,   (550)
Whill he levit, set his entencioun
To find the craft of divinacioun,
And lerit it unto the spamen all,   soothsayers
To fele before sic thingis as wald fall,
What lif, what deid, what destany and werd,
Previdit war to every man in erd.   allotted
Appollo than for his abusioun,
Whilk is the god of divinacioun,
For he usurpit in his faculte,   authority
Put him till hell, and thar remanis he.   (560)
Bot Orpheus has wone Erudices,
When our desire with resoun makis pess,
And sekis up to contemplacioun,   strives upward
Of sin detestand the abusioun.
Bot ilk man suld be war, and wisly se
That he bakwart cast noht his mindis ee
Gevand consent, and dilectacioun,
Of wardly lust for the effectioun;
For than gois bakwart to the sin agane
Our appetit, as it befor was slane   (570)
In wardly lust and sensualite,
And makis resoun wedow for to be.
Now pray we God sen our affectioun
Is allway prompe and redy to fall down,   prepared

108

That he wald helpe us with his haly hand
Of manteinans, and gif us grace to stand
In parfite luf, as he is glorius.
And thus endis the tale of Orpheus.

The Bludy Serk

This hindir yeir I hard betald   recently
Thair was a worthy king;
Dukis, erlis, and barronis bald
He had at his bidding.
The lord was anceane and ald,
And sexty yeiris couth ring;   reign
He had a dohter fair to fald,   embrace
A lusty lady ying.   (8)

Of all fairheid sho bur the flour,
And eik hir faderis air,
Of lusty laitis and he honour,   demeanour
Meik bot and debonair.
Sho winnit in a bigly bour,   pleasant bower
On fold wes none so fair;   earth
Princis luvit hir paramour
In cuntreis our allwhair.   (16)

Thair dwelt a lit beside the king
A foull giane of ane;   specially
Stollin he hes the lady ying,
Away with hir is gane,
And kest hir in his dungering,
Whair liht sho miht se nane;
Hungir and cauld and grit thristing
Sho fand into hir wane.   dwelling

He wes the laithliest on to luk   (25)
That on the ground miht gang;
His nailis wes lik ane hellis cruk,
Thairwith five quarteris lang.
Thair wes nane that he ourtuk,

In riht or yit in wrang,
Bot all inshondir he thame shuke—
The giane wes so strang. (32)

He held the lady day and niht
Within his deip dungeoun;
He wald noht gif of hir a siht,
For gold nor yit ransoun,
Bot gife the king miht get a kniht
To feht with his persoun—
To feht with him both day and niht
Whill ane wer dungin doun. beaten

The king gart seik baith fer and neir, (41)
Beth be se and land,
Of ony kniht gife he miht heir
Wald feht with that giand.
A worthy prince that had no peir
Hes tane the deid on hand,
For the luve of the lady cleir,
And held full trew cunnand. skill

That prince come proudly to the town (49)
Of that giane to heir,
And fauht with him his awin persoun,
And tuke him presoneir;
And kest him in his awin dungeoun,
Allane withouttin feir, companion
With hungir, cauld and confusioun,
As full weill worthy weir. (56)

Sine brak the bour, had hame the briht,
Unto hir fadir deir;
Sa evill wondit was the kniht
That he behuvit to de.
Unlusum was his likame diht, body, clothed
His sark was all bludy; shirt

In all the warld was thair a wiht
So peteouss for to sy?   (64)

The lady murnit and maid grit mone
With all hir mekle miht:
'I luvit never lufe bot one,
That dulfully now is diht.   woefully
God sen my life were fra me tone,
Or I had sene yone siht,
Or ellis in begging ever to gone
Furth with yone curtass kniht!'   (72)

He said, 'Fair lady, now mone I
De, trestly ye me trow;   truly
Tak ye my sark that is bludy,
And hing it forrow you;   before
First think on it and sine on me,
When men cumis you to wow.'
The lady said, 'Be Mary fre,
Thairto I mak a vow!'   (80)

When that sho lukit to the serk,
Sho thoht on the persoun,
And prayit for him with all hir harte,
That lousd hir of bandoun,   durance
Whair sho was wont to sit full merk
In that deip dungeoun;
And evir whill sho wes in quert,   alive
That wass hir a lessoun.
                                                        (88)

Sa weill the lady luvit the kniht,
That no man wald sho tak.
Sa suld we do our God of miht
That did all for us mak;
Whilk fullely to deid wes diht
For sinfull manis saik;
So suld we do both day and niht,
With prayaris to him mak.   (96)

Moralitas

This king is lik the Trinity,
Baith in hevin and heir;   *here*
The manis saule to the lady,
The giane to Lucefeir,
The kniht to Christ that deit on tre
And coft our sinnis deir,   *redeemed*
The pit to hell with panis fell,
The sin to the woweir.   (104)

The lady was wowd, bot sho said nay
With men that wald hir wed;
Sa suld we writh all sin away   *drive*
That in our breistis bred.
I pray to Jesu Christ verrey,   *himself*
For us his blud that bled,
To be our help on Domisday,
Whair lawis are straitly led.   *executed*

The saule is Godis dohtir deir,   (113)
And eik his handewerk,
That was betrasit with Lucifeir   *betrayed*
Wha sittis in hell full merk.
Borrowit with Christis angell cleir,
Hend men, will ye noht herk?   *good*
For his lufe that boht us deir,
Think on the bludy serk.   (120)

Ane Prayer For the Pest

O eterne God of power infinit,
To whois hie knawlege na thing is obscure—
That is, or was, or sal be, is perfit
Into thy siht whill that this warld indure—
Haif mercy of us, indigent and peure!
Thou dois na wrang to puneiss our offens;

113

O lord, that is to mankind haill succure,
Preserve us fra this perrelus pestilens!

perfect

(8)

We the beseik, O Lord of lordis all,
Thy eiris incline and heir our grit regrait!
We ask remeid of the in generall,
That is of help and confort desolait;
Bot thou with reuth our hairtis recreat,
We ar bot deid but only thy clemens:
We the exhort on kneis law prostrait,
Preserf us fra this perrellus pestilens!

remedy

revive

(16)

We ar riht glaid thou puneis our trespass
Be ony kind of uthir tribulatioun,
Wer it thy will, O Lord of hevin! Allais
That we sould thus be haistely put down,
And die as beistis without confessioun,
That nane dar mak with uthir residence!
O blissit Jesu that woir the thorny crown,
Preserve us frome this perrelus pestilens!

(24)

Use derth, O Lord, or seiknes and hungir soir,
And slaik thy plaig that is so penetrive!
Thy pepill ar perreist: wha ma remeid thairfoir,
Bot thou, O Lord, that for thame lost thy live?
Suppois our sin be to the pungitive,
Oure deid ma nathing our sinnis recompens.
Haif mercy, Lord; we ma not with the strive:
Preserve us frome this perrelus pestilens!

cruel

vexatious

(32)

Haif mercy, Lord; haif mercy, hevinis King!
Haif mercy of thy pepill penetent;
Haif mercy of our petous punissing;
Retreit the sentence of thy just jugement
Aganis us sinnaris that servis to be shent!
Without mercy we ma mak no defens:
Thou that, but reuth, upoun the rude was rent,
Preserve us frome this perrellus pestilens!

withdraw

punished

(40)

114

Remember, Lord, how deir thou hes us boht,   *redeemed*
That for us sinnaris shed thy pretius blude,
Now to redeme that thou hes maid of noht,
That is of vertew barrane and denude;
Haif reuth, Lord, of thine awin similitude;   *likeness*
Puneis with pety and noht with violens!
We knaw it is for our ingratitude
That we ar puneist with this pestilens.   (48)

Thou grant us grace for till amend our miss
And till evaid this crewall suddane deid;
We knaw our sin is all the cause of thiss,
For oppin sin thair is set no remeid;
The justice of God mon puneiss than bot dreid,   *without fail*
For by the law he will with non dispens;
Whair justice laikis, thair is eternall feid
Of God that sould preserf fra pestilens.   (56)

Bot wald the heiddismen that sould keip the law   *leaders*
Pueneiss the peple for thair transgressioun,
Thair wald na deid the peple than ourthraw;
Bot thay ar gevin so planely till oppressioun
That God will noht heir thair intercessioun;
Bot all ar puneist for thair innobediens
Be sword or deid, withouttin remissioun,
And hes just cause to send us pestilens.   (64)

Superne Lucerne, guberne this pestilens;   *control*
Preserve and serve that we not sterve thairin!
Decline that pine be thy devine pridens!   *diminish*
O Treuth, haif reuth; lat not our slewth us twin!   *sloth*
Our sit full tit, wer we contrit, wald blin.   *suffering, quickly,*
Dissiver did never whaevir the besoht.   *cast away* [*cease*
Send grace with space, and us imbrace fra sin!
Latt noht be tint that thou so deir hes boht!   (72)

O Prince preclair, this cair cotidiane,   *daily*
We the exhort, distort it in exile!   *turn aside*

115

Bot thou remeid, this deid is bot ane trane   snare
For to dissaif the laif, and thame begile;   others
Bot thou sa wyiss devyiss to mend this bile,   outbreak
Of this mischeif wha ma releif us oht—
For wrangus win bot thou our sin oursill?   hide
Lat noht be tint that thou so deir hes boht!   (80)

Sen for our vice that justice mon correct,
O King most hie, now pacify thy feid!   enmity
Our sin is huge; refuge we not suspect.   despair of
As thou art juge, deluge us of this dreid;   remove
In time assent or we be shent with deid
We us repent and time mispent forthoht;   misused
Thairfoir evimoir be gloir to thy godheid:
Lat noht be tint that thou sa deir hes boht!   (88)

The Thre Deid-Pollis

O sinfull man, into this mortall se
Whilk is the vaill of murning and of cair,
With gaistly siht behold oure heidis thre,
Oure holkit ene, oure peilit pollis bair!   hollow, flayed
As ye ar now into this warld we wair,
Als freshe, als fair, als lusty to behald;
Whan thou lukis on this suth examplair
Of thyself, man, thou may be riht unbald.   fearful

For suth it is that every man mortall   (9)
Mon suffer deid, and de that life hes tane;
Na erdly stait aganis deid ma prevaill.
The hour of deth and place is uncertane,
Whilk is referrit to the hie God allane;
Heirfoir haif mind of deth, that thou mon die.
This fair exampill to se quotidiane   daily
Sould caus all men fra wicket vicis fle.   (16)

116

O wantone youth, als freshe as lusty May,
Farest of flowris renewit whit and reid,
Behald our heidis! O lusty gallandis gay,
Full laihly thus sall lie thy lusty heid,   *lowly*
Holkit and how and wallowit as the weid;   *empty, withered*
Thy crampand hair and eik thy cristall ene
Full cairfully conclud sall dulefull deid;
Thy example heir be us it may be sene.   (24)

O ladeis whit, in claithis corruscant   *bright*
Poleist with perle and mony pretius stane;
With palpis whit, and hals so elegant,
Sirculit with gold and sapheris mony ane;
Your fingearis small, whit as whailis bane,
Arrayit with ringis and mony rubeis reid—
As we lie thus, so sall ye lie ilk ane
With peilit pollis, and holkit thus your heid.   (32)

O wofull prid, the rute of all distres,
With humill hairt upoun our poliss penss!
Man, for thy miss ask mercy with meikness;   *sin*
Aganis deid na man may mak defenss.
The empriour for all his excellenss,
King and quene, and eik all erdly stait,
Peure and riche, sal be but differenss
Turnit in ass and thus in erd translait.   *dust*

This questioun wha can obsolve lat see—   (41)
What phisnamour of perfit palwester: *physiognomist, palmist*
Wha was farest or foulest of us thre?
Or whilk of us of kin was gentillar?
Or maist excellent in science or in lare,
In art, musik, or in astronomye?
Heir sould be your study and repair;
And think as thus all your heidis mon be.   (48)

O febill aige, ay drawand neir the dait
Of dully deid, and hes thy dayis compleit,

117

Behald our heidis with murning and regrait!
Fall on thy kneis; ask grace at God greit
With oritionis and haly salmes sweit,
Beseikand him on the to haif mercy,
Now of our saulis bidand the decreit   decree
Of his godheid, when he sall call and cry.   (56)

Als we exhort that every man mortall,
For his saik that maid of noht all thing,
For our saulis to pray in general
To Jesus Christ, of hevin and erd the king,
That throuh his blude we may ay leif and ring
With the hie Fader be eternity,
The Sone alswa, the Haly Gaist conding,
Thre knit in ane be perfit unity.   (64)

The Prais of Aige

Within a garth, under a rede rosere,   garden, rose-tree
Ane ald man and decrepit herd I sing.
Gay was the note, swete was the voce and clere;
It was grete joy to here of sik a thing.
'And to my dome,' he said, in his diting,   opinion
'For to be yong I wald not, for my wis
Of all this warld to mak me lord and king:
The more of age the nerar hevinnis blis.   (8)

'False is this warld and full of variance,
Besouht with sin and other sitis mo;   sorrows
Treuth is all tint, gyle has the gouvernance,   lost
Wrechitnes has wroht all welthis wele to wo;
Fredome is tint and flemit the lordis fro,   driven away
And covatise is all the cause of this;
I am content that youthede is ago:
The more of age the nerar hevinnis blisse.   (16)

'The state of youth I repute for na gude,
For in that state sik perilis now I see;
Bot full smal grace, the regeing of his blude
Can none gainstand whill that he agit be;
Sine of the thing that tofore joyit he
Nothing remainis for to be callit his;
Forwhy it were bot veray vanitee:
The more of age the nerar hevinnis blisse.   (24)

'Suld no man traist this wrechit warld, forwhy
Of erdly joy ay sorow is the end;
The state of it can no man certify,
This day a king, tomorne na gude to spend.
What have we here bot grace us to defend?
The whilk God grant us for to mend oure mis,
That to his glore he may oure saulis send;
The more of age the nerar hevinnis blisse.'   (32)

NOTES

The Testament of Cresseid

Text: British Library C. 21, c. 14, unique copy of the edition printed by Henry Charteris, Edinburgh, 1593.

5. The sun leaves Aries, the sign of the Ram, on the 11th of April, the middle month of spring.

39-70. Having summarised events in Chaucer's *Troilus and Criseyde* from V,1030 onwards, Henryson refers to *ane uther quair* as his source for Cresseid's later fate. It is probably a poetic fiction, allowing Henryson to affect objective detachment from his emotive narrative and providing an ironic perspective, as in his disclaimer (64-8) of responsibility for its veracity in relation to Chaucer's account. It also justifies such changes as Troilus' survival to write Cresseid's epitaph (602-9) and the conversion of Calchas from priest of Apollo to the service of Venus (106-9).

141-266. For his portraits of the planets, Henryson seems to have drawn selectively on Boccaccio's *De Genealogia Deorum* (see MacQueen, 46-9). By making Venus, as well as Cupid, blind (135, 283), he evokes the courtly literature tradition which equated her with Fortune (see Stearns, 89-92), equally indiscriminate and changeable in her influence on the lives of men.

211-17. The horses who draw the chariot of the sun derive their names from Ovid's *Metamorphoses*, ii, 153-5: Eous, Aethon, Pyroeis and Phlegon.

261-3. Folk legend interprets the man in the moon as a peasant banished there for stealing the bundle of thorns he carries on his back.

316-43. In conformity with contemporary belief in astrological influence on human affairs, the traditional characteristics of the planets are reflected in the punishment of Cresseid's violation of the moral and physical laws of the universe. After her rejection of Venus, the moisture and heat associated with the sanguine temperament are replaced by the dry coldness of the melancholic Saturn, despiser of women, patron of beggars, source of fevers and, in union with the disparate Luna (Cynthia), of leprosy (see Elliott, 152-3). The symptoms of the disease given here and elsewhere in

121

the poem would be familiar to readers in Scotland where leprosy survived into the sixteenth century (see Fox (1968), 24-8).

379-406, 470-83. If, as suggested (S.T.S. I, 50), there was a spittal house in Dunfermline, the characteristic details of the isolation of the leper colony *at the townis end*, the provision of alms in kind for their support, their begging at the town gate, and the clapper or covered dish which they rattled as a sign of their uncleanness, no doubt derive from Henryson's own observation.

550. Henryson takes up Chaucer's frequent references to the influence on lovers of Fortune's wheel whose fickle movement brings about that fall from felicity to misery which constitutes the medieval concept of tragedy (*cf.* 4.).

582-3, 589-91. Henryson takes from Chaucer the ring given by Troilus to Criseyde (III, 1368) and his parting gift, the brooch which she later gave to Diomede (V, 1040, 1660-94). He may have added the belt because he took *broche* to mean 'buckle', or, with ironic intention, as a symbolic girdle of chastity (see S.T.S. I, 52).

The Morall Fabillis of Esope the Phrygian

Text: National Library of Scotland, unique copy of the edition printed by Thomas Bassandyne, Edinburgh, 1571. The whole consists of a prologue and thirteen Fables, seven derived from the Aesopic tradition through the Latin verse *Romulus* of Gualterus Anglicus (?*c*. 1175), most probably known to Henryson in its derivative, the thirteenth-century French *Isopet de Lyon*, and six from the medieval beast-epic, the *Roman de Renart*. Henryson has freely adapted and expanded his originals.

28. From the opening lines of Anglicus: 'The representation of solemn things wears a sweeter smile than that of humorous things'.

173. Satirical allusion to the merchant guilds who, having gained control of Scottish burgh councils, paid neither the *magna custuma* on wool, etc. nor the *parva custuma* on market goods (see MacQueen, 123-4).

248. Good Friday implies fasting and Easter Day feasting.

360. *but and ben*: outer and inner rooms of a Scottish dwelling-house.

429. *Lowrence*: more commonly 'Lowrie', perhaps 'lurker'

(*cf. lour,* v. 'to skulk').

621-2. Thetis, a sea-goddess, entertaining Phoebus implies that the sun had sunk beneath the waves.

631-41. The spheres were imagined as transparent globes encircling the earth and bearing the heavenly bodies, whose positions in relation to the divisions of the Zodiac here allow the learned fox to predict his own fate. Hence his impulse to confess his sins (see MacQueen, 145-7).

661-2. *Widdinek*: one hanged by a rope of withies or willow fronds; *Crakraip*: one likely to break the gallows rope.

667. *Waitskaith*: one who lies in wait to do harm.

704-6. To be valid the sacrament of Penance requires contrition, confession and acceptance of punishment, such as a penitential diet of fish (*cf*. 723-5).

887-90. The minotaur, offspring of Pasiphae and a bull, is as much a *beist of bastardry* as the three-headed Chimaera—here mistakenly given the name of Bellerophon, who killed it with the help of Pegasus controlled by a golden bit, the gift of Minerva; hence, perhaps, *be assent of sorcery*.

1033. From Erasmus, *Adagiorum Collectanea* (1508): 'Happy is the man whom another's perils render cautious'.

1146-1201. The supreme *prudence* of God consists in having all time, past, present and future, eternally in his sight. The concept, stated by Boethius in *De Consolatione Philosophiae* V, Prosa 6, and the influence of scholastic philosophy, have shaped Henryson's view of the harmony of the universe as a reflection of the wisdom and goodness of the Creator. The image of the bat's eye is from Aristotle, *Metaphysics* I, M. i. 3 (see MacQueen, 158-60).

1214. *Copia temporis*: a personification of the season of plenty.

1278. The second line of one of Cato's Distichs (II. 24): 'Anticipate events which are to come, and consider that they will have to be borne; for whatever we see in advance does us less harm' (Burrow, 34).

The Tale of Orpheus and Erudices his Quene

Text : Transcript of the Asloan MS. (*c.* 1515), Malahide, Dublin. The subject-matter and its basic interpretation derive from Boethius'

De Consolatione III, Metrum 12, the detailed allegorisation from the commentary on Boethius by Nicholas Trevet (?1258-1328), an English Dominican theologian (*cf.* 415-24; see MacQueen, 27-8). Henryson also makes use of details from oral tradition which celebrate Orpheus as the archetypal minstrel, prophet of Christ's coming, and as the Good Shepherd (see Louis, 643-5).

29-63. In making Orpheus the son of Apollo and the muse Calliope, and Calliope the daughter of Jupiter and Memoria, Henryson is following the common mythological tradition of his age. His more abstruse account of her sister muses seems to have been derived from the early 13th-century *Graecismus* of Eberhard of Béthune, a compendium of mythological information (see Wright, 42-5).

188. *Wadling Streit*: Watling Street, here used as a name for the Milky Way.

219-42. His experience of the music of the spheres may be intended to express the imposition of intellectual discipline on Orpheus' art in preparation for his success in charming the gods of Hell. The passage also allows Henryson to display his encyclopedic knowledge in a catalogue of Latin and Greek musical terms, many of which have been distorted in transmission (see MacQueen, 39-43).

247-344. Henryson's Hell is an anachronistic mixture of the classical and Christian underworlds, a place of unsatisfied and uncontrolled appetite, localised in the topography of Scotland. Ixion, Tantalus and Tityos suffer various tortures of insatiable desire; the catalogue of pagan and Christian rulers includes many who abused their offices and failed in their duty as moral and spiritual leaders (see MacQueen, 35-8).

The Bludy Serk

Text: The Bannatyne MS. (1568), National Library of Scotland. Resembles in narrative outline the tale of Emperor Frederick's daughter in the *Gesta Romanorum*, a popular compendium of short stories in Latin prose which Henryson may have known in an English version (see S.T.S. I, lix-lxiii).

Ane Prayer for the Pest

Text: Bannatyne MS. Outbreaks of plague in Scotland during

Henryson's lifetime were too frequent to allow the poem to be dated by association with a particular epidemic. Interpretation of such visitations as divine retribution for man's sins was a medieval commonplace.

The Thre Deid-Pollis

Text: Bannatyne MS. It is there ascribed to Patrick Johnstoun, named by Dunbar in his *Lament for the Makaris*; but metrical and stylistic features support the ascription to Henryson in the Maitland Folio MS. (*c.* 1570-85), Pepysian Library, Magdalene College, Cambridge. The death's-head was a familiar *memento mori*, warning of man's mortality and the vanity of earthly pleasures.

The Prais of Aige

Text: Chepman and Myllar Prints (1508), National Library of Scotland.